Ouuy ao   ...
love
Mayaxx

The Aylesbury Railway

An engraving by J. C. Bourne depicting rocks being blasted at Linslade in October 1837.

The Aylesbury Railway

The First Branch Line
Cheddington ~ Aylesbury

Bill Simpson

Oxford Publishing Co.

A FOULIS-OPC Railway Book

© 1989 Bill Simpson & Haynes Publishing Group

British Library Cataloguing in Publication Data
Simpson, Bill, *1940–*
    The Aylesbury railway – the first branch line.
    1. Buckinghamshire. Railway services. London and Birmingham railway. Cheddington – Aylesbury line, history
    I. Title
    385'.09425'9

    ISBN .i.0-86093-438-1

Library of Congress Catalog Card Number
    89-84716

Published by:
Haynes Publishing Group
Sparkford, Near Yeovil, Somerset. BA22 7JJ

Haynes Publications Inc.
861 Lawrence Drive, Newbury Park, California 91320, USA.

Printed by: J.H. Haynes & Co. Ltd

Acknowledgements

To the following I should like to convey my gratitude for the very kind assistance and support so freely given in order to enable me to compile this history.

Mike Crosbie who helped with research, in particular the line drawings of structures.

Geoff Williams, Bob and Mike Williams who researched exhaustively on the branch long before it was known by me.

The late Bill George (Councillor), Jack Turner, LCGB (Bedford Branch), Ken Hall, Len Kinchen, Cyril Gibbins, John Lowe, Mr Elliott Viney, Fred Cockman, Mr F.A. Goodyer, Ron Miller, Mr J.P. Mullett, Mrs McLees, Mr R.

Pallet, Mr A.M. Perry, John Spencer, Arthur Waller, Geoff Webb, John Sharland, Mr D. Mason, Mr R.H. Thompkins, Mrs Wilkins, Wesley Robins.

Also the following essential sources and staff who answered every request with patience and diligent help.

Bucks. County Library (Buckinghamshire Collection).
Bucks. County Museum.
Bucks. County Record Office.
Public Record Office, Kew.
BPCC Hazell, Watson & Viney Limited.
Nestlé Company Limited.

Bibliography

The Aylesbury Railway E.J.S. Gadsden.
Railway Development at Aylesbury '1' G. Machell, B.Sc.,Ph.D., A.R.I.C.
Forgotten Railways, Chilterns & Cotswolds R. Davies & M.D. Grant.
The Aylesbury Branch, by Bob Williams, British Railway Journal.
Herepath's Railway Magazine, 1836.
Herepath's Railway Magazine, July 1839.
Bucks. Herald.
Bucks. Free Press.

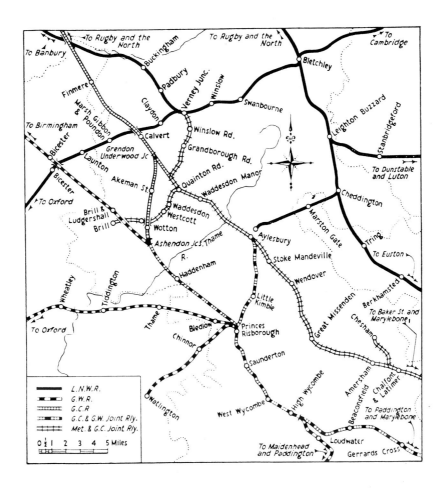

Preface

The unique feature of the Aylesbury Branch is perhaps that it has no particular feature of special significance. There are no earthworks of note, nor tunnels and the only bridge over the line was a footbridge. Few lines are so geometrically straight and but for short sections at each end it appears, amidst the railway map of Buckinghamshire, like the precise stroke of a draughtsman's pen.

Its true individuality lies in its origins, being within the initial stages of the first generation of railway building. Few lines carry on their documents of Royal Assent the cypher of William IV.

Although it was not intended initially as a single track rural branch line it can probably claim to be the first, or very near, of that widespread and much loved impecunious breed. Not that the Aylesbury line did not prove lucrative. Its creators profited by it and under the subsequent ownership of the LNWR it enjoyed a monopoly of the town's railway needs for a total of 25 years.

The arrival of the GWR in Aylesbury did little to affect the existing services of the LNWR, apart from forcing them to dig into their pockets and build a better station!

As a quarter of the capital for the line was subscribed locally it cannot be doubted that the civic leaders and businessmen of Aylesbury were prepared to speak in money as well as words when they described their enthusiasm to be joined with the new main line of the London & Birmingham Railway. Unfortunately the opportunity to exploit their clear advantage and reach Oxford by 1840 was ill served by subsequent misfortune and faltered on several other occasions. Nevertheless the line saw intensive use in its truncated form, moreover, the goods traffic service ended with some reluctance from a number of local industries when that turbulent railway decade of the 1960s saw it brought to an end.

During 1989 thoughts will be focussed on the 150th anniversary of the opening of which, hopefully, this book will renew the memory of an almost forgotten first branch line.

Bill Simpson
Banbury

Contents

Robert Stephenson as a young man and likely to be during the period of the building of the London & Birmingham Railway. The locomotive drawing appears to be a relative of the long-boilered type but in this case with inside cylinders. Although in his early years he developed the steam locomotive along with his father, it is with great civil engineering achievements of railway works that he is best known.

National Railway Museum

Chapter 1

Outline History

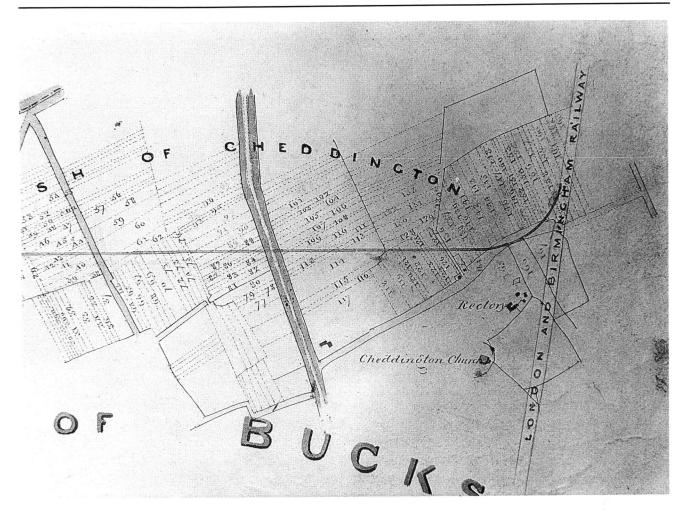

Curve of the line swinging away from the path of the yet unrealised London & Birmingham Railway.

Bucks Public Record Office

The first proposal for a railway from London to Birmingham was by the famous canal builder John Rennie. He commissioned a survey which placed the terminus in Islington, alongside the Regent's Canal. From there it went north to Harrow, Rickmansworth, Watford, Hemel Hempstead, Cheddington, Quainton, Brackley, Southam (with a tunnel under the Oxford Canal), continuing to two miles short of Coventry. The strong opposition of landowning interests in those early days made sure that the plan foundered. Interestingly a route favoured by George Stephenson went from Uxbridge and along the Misbourne Valley to Aylesbury. This would have been cheaper with less excavation. Leading opponents like the Duke of Buckingham saw to it that the scheme failed and it would be another 76 years before a main line railway would in fact take the same route.

The opposition could however only forestall what was inevitable, for it would only be a matter of time before a railway would be built between the Capital and the second city, whosoever opposed it.

Another survey of 1829 proposed what would later be a Great Western Railway path, via Oxford and Banbury. This was countered by a strong lobby in favour of persevering with the direct route. In a climate of reason that would have better sustained railway progress in the subsequent 'mania' years, all opinions polarised into the representation of an eight-person committee that would appoint George and Robert Stephenson as engineers to survey and build the new line. George probably felt that this was his son's great opportunity and later stepped aside to allow him full control. The salary for the work was to be £1,500 per annum which proved to be well earned by subsequent events.

The first Stephenson terminus was situated near the Edgware Road instead of in Islington, but after taking another survey in 1831 he decided on Euston, although

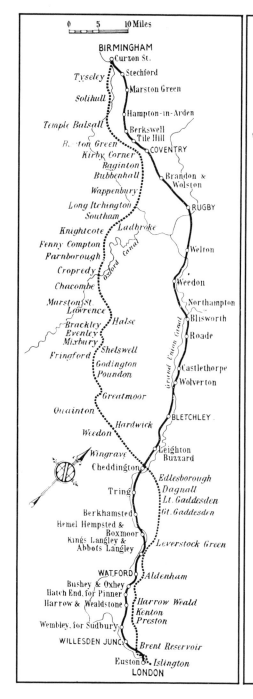

AYLESBURY RAILWAY.

FIVE POUNDS REWARD.

Some evil-disposed Person or Persons have lately *feloniously Stolen and carried away*, a quantity of RAILS, STAKES, and MATERIALS, belonging to the Company, for which any Offender, on Conviction, is liable to Transportation for Seven Years.

Several STAKES driven into the Ground for the purpose of setting out the Line of Railway, *have also been Pulled up and Removed*, by which a Penalty of Five Pounds for each Offence has been incurred, half Payable to the Informer and half to the Company.

The above Reward will be paid on Conviction, in addition to the Penalty, to any Person who will give Evidence sufficient to Convict any Offender guilty of either of the above Crimes, on application to Mr. HATTEN or Mr. ACTON TINDAL, of Aylesbury.

By Order of the Directors.

Aylesbury, August 18th, 1838.

May, Printer, Aylesbury.

The London & Birmingham Railway as built, compared to the survey of 1824 by Sir John Rennie (broken line). Coincidentally, Cheddington complies with both routes.

Railway Magazine

A theft of rails and stakes, in 1838 when the Aylesbury Railway were busily stockpiling materials all along the route. Five pounds would certainly be an incentive to a witness for the prosecution. Note the era of founding colonies and the penalty of Transportation.

F.G. Cockman Collection

it would be necessary to operate the haulage of inclined planes between there and Camden at the top of the bank of 1 in 70 by stationary engine until 1844.

The Act for the London & Birmingham Railway received the Royal Assent on 6th May 1833, it had been estimated at a cost of £2,400,456. It was a momentous

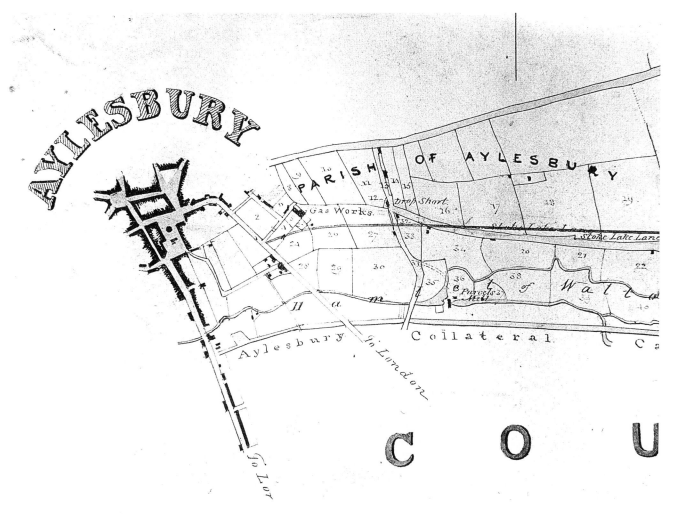

It is interesting to see the actual spot for the station site in 1835 was south of the gasworks where the later station was built. This site would be chosen in prospect of extending the lines across both London roads and on to Cheltenham or Oxford.

Bucks Public Record Office

day in railway history, for a north country company, the Grand Junction Railway, that would eventually carry the rails north of Birmingham into Lancashire, also received assent on the same day. It was a daunting challenge for Robert Stephenson, who had to pass between the two cities fifteen times either walking or by horseback to complete his survey by moon and lantern light. His surveyors were besieged, threatened and assaulted, but never dissuaded. The route now undertaken was the one familiar to this day and illustrated in this book.

The rails of this new line were initially 50lb to the yard and 16ft long with 4ft centres bearing on stone blocks. Later construction was with 65lb and 75lb per yard in 15ft lengths. Both weights were found less than satisfactory and some longer heavier rails of more conventional design were tried. Suspended fish-plate joints with transverse timber sleepering were used.

The first sod was cut at Chalk Farm on 1st June 1834, and heavy works like Primrose Hill and Watford Tunnels followed with the famous lithographs of J.C. Bourne bearing witness to the spectacular cutting at Tring. By 12th November 1834 works commenced within the neighbourhood of Newport Pagnell, where eventually the locomotive, carriage and wagon works would be built.

Whilst construction commenced on the main line a number of very interested parties in the town of Aylesbury were already alert to what was happening in the country and where future prosperity lay. Under the Chairmanship of Lord Nugent the Aylesbury Railway was formed to make a connection with this new line when it opened. The first formal meeting was held at the White Hart, Aylesbury on 10th November 1835 with amongst those present principally being Lord Nugent, Sir Harry Verney of Claydon House and Robert Stephenson. Support was not found wanting, unlike towns where established interests opposed railways such

LONDON EUSTON TO CREWE, COPPENHALL JUNCTION AND BRANCHES—*continued*

Description of Block Signalling on Main Lines (Dots indicate Block Posts)	Stations and Signal Boxes	Distance between signal boxes		Additional running lines		Loops and Refuge Sidings		Permanent speed restrictions miles per hour		Catch points, spring or unworked trailing points		Engine Whistles L—long S—short				C—crow
												Down		Up		For
		M	Yds	Up	Down	Description	Standage Wagons E. & V.	Down	Up	Position	Gradient (Rising unless otherwise shown) 1 in	Main or Fast	Slow or Goods	Main or Fast	Slow or Goods	
	CHEDDINGTON STATION TO AYLESBURY HIGH STREET STATION															
	CHEDDINGTON STATION TO AYLESBURY HIGH STREET STATION							30	30	MAXIMUM PERMISSIBLE SPEED						
●	**Cheddington Station** .. (See page 19)	—	—						15	Through junction.				1S, pause 3S		Branch to Middle Siding.
●	**Marston Gate** (Level Crossing)	2	1210							*Drivers must whistle when 1 mile distant from Mentmore Level Crossing.* *Marston Gate Level Crossing.*						
●	**Aylesbury High Street Station** (Level Crossing)	4	225							*Drivers must whistle when 1 mile distant from Broughton Level Crossing.*						

Train Staff and ticket

London Midland Region Working Appendix for 15th October 1960. The passenger service had now ceased and instructions remained for goods trains. From 3.30pm to 10.30am each weekday the gates were placed across the lines where there is no crossing keeper on duty and all signals kept at danger. At weekends this applied from 3.30pm Saturday until 10.30am Monday morning.

Cyril Gibbins Collection

as Abingdon and Oxford, there being an accommodating enthusiasm at Aylesbury. This was not without precedent, as since 1815 the town had made great use of an arm of the Grand Junction Canal to bring coals and boost the agricultural economy of the town.

A further meeting was held a month later on 5th December 1835 with the full board under the chairmanship of the local supporting banker William Medley Esq. It is interesting to compare the business interests of the investors – the astute men that saw promise in what was at that time a very rudimentary form of goods conveyance.

The Rev. C. Erle. Representing the London & Birmingham Railway.
Thos. Tindal Esq. Clerk to the Peace and Joint Secretary.
Mr Pulver.
Mr R. Harper.
Mr H. Hatton. Solicitor and Joint Secretary.
Mr D. Reid. Linen and woollen drapers.
Mr Argles.
Mr A. Lines. Grocers and tea dealers.
Mr Wm. Green. Carpenter, Joiners and Timber dealers.
Mr P. Phillips.
Mr A.O. Medley. Banker
Mr Acton Tindal. Solicitor.
Mr Ryde. The Bucks Herald newspaper.
Mr C. Williamson.
Mr W. Griffin for Mr Cox.
Mr J. Gurney. Timber dealer
Mr Mason.

Mr John Gibbs. Auctioneer, appraisers and pawn-broker.
Mr Hoare.
Mr Creed.
Mr Thomas Horwood.
Mr T. Chapman. Banker.
Mr J.K. Fowler. Proprietor of White Hart (posting lodge), Market Square.
Mr Wm. Lines.
Also in attendance was Mr Robert Stephenson.

The line had good support of the local MPs Lord Nugent and William Rickford, banker.

Estimated sum for construction was	£45,242
Parliamentary Expenses	£ 5,000
Total	£50,242

This was to be raised by 2,500 shares at £20, each with a deposit of £2 per share.

Breakdown of costs

Land – 62 acres at £150 per acre.	9,300
Excavations	4,394
Culverts	894
Accommodation bridges	3,000
Fencing	2,800
Laying and ballasting	7,000
Sleepers	4,200
Rails and chairs	9,000
Sidings and stations	2,500
	43,088
Add 5%	2,154
Total	£45,242

It must be remembered that railways as early as this thought more in terms of goods merchandise rather than passenger conveyance, this being only ten years after the opening of the Stockton & Darlington Railway and five years after the opening of the Liverpool & Manchester.

Expected produce for conveyance to London:
Butter, meat cattle, sheep, pigs, butcher's meat, hay, 5,000 ducks per week for 20 weeks, milk and cream, parcels, coaches and wagons. Passengers 15 daily. Total £255 8s 10d. (£255.44)

Produce to be brought from London:
24 tons grocery, drapery goods, ironmongery, 30 tons timber, oil cake. Passengers 15 daily. Total £118 10s (£118.50)
They enthused that passenger services would be greatly supported from Thame, Bicester, Brill, Princes Risborough, Bledlow etc.

The first mention of interest in support of the Aylesbury Railway in the L&B boardroom minutes occurs on 17th February 1836 when George Carr Glyn was chairman of the company.

With a firm prospectus and the effective support of the Marquis of Chandos and Sir Harry Verney the Aylesbury Bill was successful in parliament and received the Royal Assent on 19th May 1836. In the following June Aylesbury Railway share certificates were printed and quickly distributed to applications totalling 1,500.

During the interim period of shepherding the Bill through parliament another scheme was promoted that rivalled the Aylesbury one, the Cheltenham, Oxford & London and Birmingham Union Railway. Starting from Tring on the main line and connecting with the proposed Aylesbury route one mile from its terminus, it passed through the town and beyond, close by the famous needle making village of Long Crendon, with a branch to Oxford from Headington north of that city, before continuing on to Cheltenham where it would connect up with the Birmingham & Gloucester Railway. This scheme was brought under the study of the Aylesbury Board at a meeting on 9th March 1836. In view of the fact that the Aylesbury company did not see their line remaining as a humble branch line to Aylesbury it can be understood that they would see this interloper as an unfavourable counterstroke to their own schemes. The rival company claimed that it was providing direct connection to the spa town of Cheltenham from London. But it was just this kind of lodging of conflicting schemes and counterproposals that would bring the railways into confusion and mania a few years later.

There was a certain amount of delegatory parlying between the two camps with the ambivalent Stephenson backing both sides by surveying and speaking for each. He originally claimed that his Cheltenham Railway survey would take in the town of Aylesbury and had it remained so, in all probability the Aylesbury Railway would have become consolidated with the new scheme. Later he considered this scheme impractical and costly and that his preferred route would take the line no closer to Aylesbury than the village of Bishopstone. What would be needed then would be an extension from Aylesbury to join this line which would clearly carry the main London traffic, having serious consequences for the Aylesbury line. Whatever, the Cheltenham scheme did not draw the necessary capital for a large undertaking even after dropping the proposed branch to Oxford . Although still popular, the spa towns were beginning to feel the first effect of competing interest for the seaside, one that the railways would eventually capitalise on with enormous relish a few years later.

Rarely photographed outside the preserved state, one of the Bury 2-2-0 engines of the type which began the service on the Aylesbury Railway. Their tenure was not long after the formation of the LNWR in 1846 and they were despatched from the modest exertions of the Aylesbury line as early as 1847.

Railway Magazine

Timetable for the 1st October 1839, four months after the line had been opened. This underlines Cheddington's very minor role as a junction station which at this time was probably little more than a timber platform. Comparison with the London & Birmingham timetable on p29 suggests that for some trains coaches were split or joined at Tring, if they did not run straight through. For passengers travelling north, Tring served as a junction station as every train in both directions stopped at that station. It is interesting to see the coaches operating through to Oxford and back via Thame, this being at the time of the prospective extension of the Aylesbury Railway.

Author's Collection

AYLESBURY RAILWAY,

IN CONJUNCTION WITH THE

LONDON AND BIRMINGHAM.

Hours of Departure and Time Table, on and after 1st October, 1839.

DELAYS AT CHEDDINGTON AVOIDED.

TRAINS TO LONDON.

Leave Aylesbury.	Tring.	B. Hampstead.	Boxmoor.	Watford.	Harrow.	London.
H. M.	h. m.	h. m.	h. m.	h. m.	h. m.	h. m.
7 10 Morning ..	7 45	7 55	8 5	8 20	8 45	9 30
11 0 Morning ..	11 40	11 50	12 0	12 15	12 40	1 15
7 0 Evening ..	7 35	..	..	8 10	..	9 30

TRAINS TO AYLESBURY.

Leave London.	Harrow.	Watford.	Boxmoor.	B. Hampstead.	Tring.	Aylesbury.
H. M.	h. m.	h. m.	h. m.	h. m.	h. m.	h. m.
8 0 Morning ..	8 30	8 50	9 10	9 20	9 35	10 15
3 0 Afternoon ..	3 30	3 50	4 10	4 20	4 35	5 15
6 0 Evening ..	6 30	6 50	7 10	7 20	7 35	8 15

SUNDAY TRAINS.

Leave Aylesbury.	Tring.	B. Hampstead.	Boxmoor.	Watford.	Harrow.	London.
H. M.	h. m.	h. m.	h. m.	h. m.	h. m.	h. m.
7 10 Morning ..	7 45	7 55	8 5	8 20	8 45	9 30
4 50 Afternoon	5 30	5 40	5 55	6 5	6 30	7 30

Leave London.	Harrow.	Watford.	Boxmoor.	B. Hampstead.	Tring.	Aylesbury.
H. M.	h. m.	h. m.	h. m.	h. m.	h. m.	h. m.
8 0 Morning ..	8 30	8 50	9 10	9 20	9 35	10 15
6 0 Evening ..	6 30	6 50	7 10	7 20	7 35	8 15

Fares to and from London, 8s. 6d. First Class, & 5s. 6d. Second Class.

COACHES in connexion with this line of Railway leave Oxford, through Thame &c. at 8 o'Clock in the Morning, and 4 in the Afternoon, and forward Passengers by the ELEVEN o'Clock Morning, and SEVEN Evening Trains. Passengers are booked in LONDON throughout for Oxford, by the EIGHT o'Clock Morning, and THREE Afternoon Trains. Passengers going to Birmingham &c. and the down Road Stations, are booked to Tring, whence they will take the down Trains:—by the Train leaving Aylesbury at ELEVEN, Passengers will meet with the least delay, as the Eleven o'Clock Train from London will reach Tring at 12h. 25m. calling at First Class Stations only. Passengers from Birmingham will be booked by the Four o'Clock, and on Sunday, by the Half-past One, Afternoon Trains from thence.

Private Carriages and Horses must be at the Station at least 15 minutes before the time of departure.

Carriage Trucks and Horse Boxes are kept at the Station; but to prevent disappointment, it is requisite that notice should be given the day previous to their being required.

The Company do not hold themselves responsible for Luggage, unless booked and paid for according to its value; but, they strongly recommend all Passengers, to have their name and destination clearly stated on their luggage, and to see that it is put upon the carriage.

Parcels and Packages are forwarded as usual.

Post-horses are always in readiness at the Euston Station—Charge to any part of London, including post-boy, 10s. 6d.

OCTOBER, 1839.

[J. H. Marshall, Printer, Aylesbury.]

On the larger scene the Cheltenham proposal was an interesting foray in the developing conflict between the broad gauge (7ft $0^1/4$in) of the Great Western Railway and the 'narrow' Stephenson gauge camp (4ft $8^1/2$in). The GWR were at this time pursuing their line to Bristol and were also keen to have a Cheltenham connection. They supported a proposal for a Cheltenham & Great Western Union Railway (Cheltenham, Gloucester, Stroud, joining the main line at Swindon). Although this route of 120 miles was in excess of the L&B line of 99 miles it was able to be more effective in drawing financial support. It was granted the Royal Assent on 21st June 1836 which was in fact two months before the line to Bristol had achieved legality for its section between Paddington and West Drayton.

With the failure of the Cheltenham line its supporters joined the ranks of the Aylesbury scheme to the tune of £2,500. The Aylesbury Railway itself considered but a starting point for a much more ambitious development.

Unfortunately the first piece of bad luck to forestall the optimism was the collapse of a local bank, Medley's of Aylesbury in January 1837. They were strong supporters of the line and it caused something of a local financial panic. Much of the finance was locally based and the Aylesbury directors called a special meeting to consider whether they could fulfil their commitments to the line. They decided to proceed with the line to Aylesbury but any prospect of continuing it to Cheltenham or Oxford would have to be shelved indefinitely. The Chair for the meeting was taken for the first time by a local businessman who would feature significantly in various other railway schemes and protracted extensions in the area in later years, George Carrington. The decision was probably more momentous than was realised at the time, for had there not been the financial crisis and the plan to extend to Oxford been carried through, that city would have had its first station in the late 1830s, four years before the GWR reached it!

To give some idea of topical events taking place on the greater enterprise of the building of the main line, the L&B had suddenly found its endeavours not so compliant with the terra firma. These included the collapse of the Watford Tunnel which killed several men in 1835, and the sudden ingress of that capricious bore the $1^1/4$ mile long Kilsby Tunnel in 1836. Such a volume of watery quicksand invaded the workings that the

What must be one of the earliest photographs of a station front – 1856. Clearly defined is the new brickwork of the Aylesbury Station building, now 17 years old. Just turning on the left is the horse omnibus from the George Hotel. The more genteel landau in the centre with the crested arms on the door waits indifferently for the probable first class patron. Tall hats of the period are clearly in evidence but the main interest from the railway point of view is the gentleman standing behind the man holding the horse's bridle in the centre. He appears to be wearing a uniform with a prominent watch chain, always suggesting railway personnel. This may in some small measure suggest a porter of the period dress, a soft cap with shiny peak and fairly prominent badges on each lapel.

Bucks County Museum

OPENING OF
THE
AYLESBURY RAILWAY

The Directors propose to travel in Railway Carriages, along the line to Cheddington, twice on MONDAY Morning next, when they will be happy in the Company of such of the Shareholders with their friends as may find it convenient, who may be provided with Tickets on application to the Secretaries, on or before Saturday, the 8th Inst.

They will dine at the White Hart Inn, at Four o'clock. Tickets for which, price 10s. to include Dessert and a Bottle of Wine, may be had at the Bar of the White Hart, or of the Secretaries, on or before Saturday next. An early application for Dinner Tickets is particularly requested, as AFTER Saturday No TICKETS will be issued.

Aylesbury, 3rd June, 1839.

Notice for private celebration of the prospective opening.

Robin Pallet

hapless contractor retired in a parlous condition of health as his budget of £99,000 was rocketed to a cost of £400,000. Robert Stephenson was forced to take matters in hand himself to avoid the whole undertaking being placed in financial catastrophe. He installed powerful steam pumps which took 19 months to make the 2,432 yard tunnel workable again, which exceeded the planned opening day of the line and costing £200,000 in excess of Stephenson's estimate.

The L&B was opened as far as Boxmoor in July 1837, then Tring in October which began a London to Tring service of 1 hour 8 minutes, first class 7s 6d (37^1/2p) and second class 4s 6d (22^1/2p). The enthusiasm of Aylesbury to take advantage of this service is illustrated by the enterprising proprietor of the Bull's Head who opened a daily omnibus service over the 9^1/4 miles to Tring station on 21st October.

In the following June the local press announced that the line was now open to a place called Denbigh Hall near the village of Bletchley, there it was forced to pause as a result of the Kilsby drama. The section from Birmingham to Rugby opened on 9th April 1838.

As the main line opened further up the country it was praised by passengers, cattle farmers and graziers who relished the prospect of entraining cattle and not driving it to London markets on the hoof, which showed considerably on the weight of the beasts. Thus the railways were beginning to create their widespread effects on commerce; in this case by improving the quality of meat. On 17th September 1838 the London & Birmingham was opened throughout.

The compounded problem of Kilsby had cost the L&B dear, for as the date of Queen Victoria's Coronation drew near, on 28th June, the first great trunk line was to remain incomplete. The hiatus inspired a rodeo like event between the abutting railheads of Denbigh Hall and Rugby as every equestrian vehicle in the area was commissioned to shuttle the gap with passengers, mail and all sundry luggage and goods under the auspices of that famous coach and carrier firm, Chaplin & Horne. Such a hurling forth of hoof and wheel remained immortalised with script on stone on the wastes of Denbigh Hall long after the blasts of passing steam locomotives passed it indifferently by.

Having weathered its own crisis the Aylesbury company cut the first turf for their line on 12th May 1838. Time lost since the Royal Assent due to the bank collapse had forced a serious drain on capital. This can best be appreciated by an example of matters that had to be put in hand well before the soil had been disturbed.

In January 1838 the Aylesbury Railway Company requested tenders in the local press for "sleepers of larch oak to be cut from sound trees slowly grown, each sleeper no less than 9 feet long by 10 inches wide and 5 inches thick at centre (a profile of the end shows them tapering from the centre to about 3 inches at each edge). The sleepers for the railway are to be brought along the canal for 1st June 1838 and to be delivered to Broughton canal wharf on the Aylesbury Canal 2,000 by 1st July 1838 4,000 sleepers to be delivered to Cheddington wharf on the Grand Junction Canal. By 1st August 1838 2,000 sleepers to be delivered to Broughton wharf and by 1st September 1838; 4,000 sleepers to be delivered to Cheddington wharf. Tenders for sleepers to be submitted to Magistrates Chambers on 9th May 1838."

Thankfully there was no miniature Kilsby and contractor J.R. Chapman was able to report in July 1838 that work was progressing very fast and he thought that the line would be completed by November of the same year. In the event his estimate proved to be six months too early. Should the men have had time to glance from their labours near Cheddington they would have witnessed the wonder of the age with trains passing between London & Birmingham behind Bury engines taking about five hours to complete their journey.

As the maps and diagrams indicate the Aylesbury Railway was mainly level and straight with a climb of about 1-118 for seven furlongs before reaching the junction station on a 13 chain curve with a radius of 12 chains, a distance of 6 miles 7 furlongs and 66 yards.

There was little in way of earthworks to concern Chapman, with a slight embankment of about 365 yards followed by an equally slight cutting of just over a third of a mile near Betlow Farm which practically had the railway at its front door! There were no river or road bridges whatsoever nor any stations en route as the station for the village of Long Marston was not opened until 1860, but a gated crossing was installed with a cottage for the railway policeman (crossing keeper), another was installed at Broughton Road and another almost in the environs of Aylesbury station itself at Dropshort (Park Street). The road crossing that came to be known as Mentmore Crossing was close to the village where, in 1850, the Rothschild estate and building of a large house took place.

The line was built in the spirit and practical consideration of eventually being extended further and requiring an 'up' and 'down' line, so space was allocated for two sets of rails.

A feature of construction was control of budget expenditure. It ran over its original estimate of £50,000 to £59,000, but was reasonably contained as subsequent events proved.

Under the terms of the Act the L&B undertook to rent the line from 15th January 1840 for £2,500 per annum being the rate of 5 per cent per annum on the estimated outlay (Aylesbury having to stand the extra £9,000). The owning company were totally responsible for the permanent way for the first twelve months.

At the outset the L&B had intended to own only the lines and hire out their use on a toll system like turnpikes and canals had done. However, capital funding for feeder branches, improvements in the permanent way and reliable locomotives and rolling stock meant an extension of the undertaking to form a complete railway company in the accepted sense.

After the line had been in operation for some six years the interests of the L&B were undertaken by the new company of the London & North Western Railway, largely as an amalgam of the L&B, Grand Junction, Liverpool & Manchester and Manchester & Birmingham Railways, establishing a company that would eventually own the route from London to Carlisle. This incorporation took place on 16th July 1846 and included the purchase of the Aylesbury Railway for £60,000 which in effect ensured that those enterprising men of Aylesbury had indeed exacted a justifiable bargain.

Returning to the opening of the Aylesbury Railway, the feted day for public opening had been set for 10th June 1839, a month after J.R. Chapman had confidently entrained a party of directors and friends along the branch and back in a dozen carriages. Thus far all was considered ready to accept business.

On the morning of the opening the sun was shining brightly at the appointed time of launching of the first train, 7 o'clock. To the engine was attached five elegant first class carriages and three of the second class. The first trip to Cheddington was accomplished in 14

Seal of the Aylesbury Railway Company.

Bucks County Museum

minutes to cover the seven miles. The engineer for the project did not wish, understandably, to forego the opportunity to regale the company with the breathtaking potential of the new railway when he stated. "It could take five minutes at 84 miles an hour or seven minutes at 60 miles an hour." Presumably he also considered the prospect in his average, of bringing the train to a halt at each end, especially in view of the less considered topic of train braking!

However, it was a day for exaggerated praise and hyperbole with the departure of each train being accorded the refrains of the Long Crendon village band in no mean style. Thousands crowded around the station as the small station platform could barely accommodate more than the regulation admission right of holding a shareholder's ticket.

Appropriate to these occasions arrangements were made for a large banquet at the White Hart Hotel where a company of 80 gentlemen sat down to dinner. The speech for the Chair was made by Thomas Tindal Esq., in absence of the Chairman George Carrington of Missenden. Mr Tindal pointed out that one quarter of the shares were subscribed locally. Further to regale the ears not only of the directors but a section representing the Board of the L&B, George Carrington arrived and spoke of the following. "Prior to the railway opening the only means of travelling to London had been by coach which left Aylesbury at 6 o'clock in the morning arriving in London at 10 o'clock in the evening, 14 hours travelling. By use of the Aylesbury Railway this will now be two hours."

Indeed there was much for Aylesbury to celebrate. The town had become the county town of the County of

Medal struck commemorating the opening of the Aylesbury **Railway** on 10th June 1839. Note R. Stephenson Esq. Engineer. The head side ennobles the Chairman, George Carrington Esq.

Geoff Williams

Buckingham and had achieved a distinction as yet unknown to the other county towns of Bedford and Oxford. The air must have been heady with congratulations, every shop was closed and the townspeople were given a full day's holiday to experience the delectation of either riding the rails themselves to Cheddington and back, or watching this wonder of horseless movement take place. The summer twilight was filled with the flashes and bangs of a fireworks display adding a crystalline gaiety to the scene below. Banquet speeches affirmed the confidence shown in the undertaking, repeating the prophecy of those with the foresight to realize what railway connection would mean to towns in the future.

". . . there can be little doubt that branches from the chief towns and districts on each side of the line will be formed to the diffusion of benefits throughout the kingdom, and to the special advantage of the proprietors of this company, by whose main road along the communication with the metropolis must be maintained." There is the irony of unforeseen disappointment in these words, for having so successfully made that first step to a larger undertaking the Aylesbury line faltered several times until it was overtaken by competing schemes and it lost that early initiative, never to be regained.

The sobriety of regular train running came on Tuesday morning 11th June when the first fare paying passengers boarded the first timetable trains. There were three trains on each weekday and two on Sundays, connecting with London trains at Cheddington for a 43 mile journey to the Capital in 2 hours 10 minutes at a cost of 8s 6d (42^1/2p) first class and 5s 6d (27^1/2p) second class. There appears to be no provisions for a third class. Although the fare was not cheap, a labourer's wages were about 6s 0d (30p) a week, nevertheless, 260 persons availed themselves of the service in the first week; on the second week 229; the third week 290 and after an amazing rise to 419 on the fourth week the total for the month became 1,199.

The opening of the Aylesbury line brought an additional stopping train on the main line between Cheddington and Euston – a 2^1/2 hour journey. Goods trains began regular workings in November which awakened the canal owners to the competition for which they would have to compete with keener priced tolls. But the station at Aylesbury was by no means equipped to make serious incursions into canal wharfage.

Fortunately an account of this early railway was published in Whishaw's *Railways of Great Britain & Ireland* (1842). It is an absolute gem to railway students, to have sufficient first hand detail of how an early branch line appeared. Together with the diagram of the same period it is possible to gather fairly clear indication of how it all must have looked.

Up to December 31st, 1839, the following sums had been paid for works, &c. : —

Earthworks, ballasting, and permanent-way materials, &c.	£18,829 10 10
Rails	6900 0 0
Chairs and turn-tables	3400 0 0
Sleepers	3709 3 0
Land and compensation	9046 19 3
Stations	934 15 7
Parliamentary Expenses	2620 17 2
Engineering, including surveyor's charges	1962 11 6
Law charges	964 12 6
Advertisements, printing, and stationery	453 0 2
Secretary's expenses	125 0 0
Interest on loans, &c.	138 13 10
	£49,085 3 10
Existing liabilities	9914 16 2
Total cost of railway	£59,000 0 0

Thus, the excess over the parliamentary estimate is 13,758*l.*

This railway was laid out and executed under the general direction of Mr. Robert Stephenson; and the works throughout appear to be constructed in a substantial, and at the same time in an economical manner.

Even a cursory observation will reveal a naivety in layout. From the viewpoint of nearly 150 years later, after the great age of the network passed through its most resourceful development, it seems primitive to say the least. Nevertheless it should be regarded within the limitations of the time to be advantageous enough. A familiar sight is the liberal displacement of turntables for moving stock and not just turning locomotives. The scarcity of the latter meant that they were fully employed hauling trains from one point to another whilst the shunting and movement of stock was down to the muscle of man and horse. Also, the fitting of goods vehicles with end loading facilities or one-side loading only seems incomprehensibly awkward. One cannot avoid the impression that work was physically hard long after the last railway navvy had left the site!

"The rails are chiefly of the parallel form, similar to those used on the London & Birmingham Railway, they are in 16 feet lengths and fixed in chairs by means of wooden keys, the chairs are placed 4 feet from centre to centre along the line of railway; the sleepers are from 9 to 10 feet in length, and of full scantling. Open lateral drains, and cross tile-drains 6^1/$_2$ inches internal diameter, add greatly to the security of the works.

The station at Aylesbury is conveniently laid out: a triple way, connected, at a convenient distance from the offices, with the main line, runs into a railway dock 33 feet wide at its entrance, and 12 feet at its connection with the terminal turntable, the side space of which is 4 feet 10 inches; the height of the quay, which has a curved batter (retaining wall wider at the bottom than at the top) of 2^3/$_4$ inches is 3 feet 4 inches; the quay on either side is about 10 feet in width. There is a carriage dock 10 feet 8 inches in length, and 8 feet 10 inches wide, furnished at its entrance with a proper turntable, and abutting on the yard, conveniently situate for the arrival of common-road vehicles; the arrival door for the passengers is at the booking office, on the left side of the railway as you approach Aylesbury; the departure gate is on the right side; for the whole of the station there is a siding for carriages when not in use.

The booking office and general waiting room are in one; there is however, a separate room for ladies. This is, upon the whole, one of the best arranged stations for a short line railway that we have anywhere met with. There is a locomotive engine house at each end of the line: (reference to a locomotive engine house at Cheddington is intriguing as this provokes interest on how engine rostering was worked): *that at Aylesbury is about 100 feet in length, and 16 feet in clear width. On the top of this building is a capacious tank for the supply of water for the locomotives."*

Locomotives and stock were hired to the company under the Act of the L&B who supplied two small Bury 2-2-0s for the purpose. In a salutory way these were called *Aylesbury No. 1* and *Aylesbury No. 2*. Early locomotives were often named after the lines they

The railway policeman or 'Bobby' as he was known with his semaphore indication of red and white flags during the day, and white, green and red lamp for night to control train movement. On the main line they were stationed at fixed intervals (1 – 1^1/$_2$ miles) but on the branch they manned only the road crossings.

National Railway Museum

worked. In 1838 two Bury engines on the Manchester-Bolton line were named *Manchester* and *Bolton*. Although ideal for use on the branch such engines were soon to find their limitations on the main line. Especially when the broad gauge GWR opened their route to Birmingham via Oxford and started to outstrip L&B times with the introduction of Gooch's famous 'Highflyers'. Indeed the Bury engine's time on the

The original Aylesbury station of the branch from the London & Birmingham Railway. It is believed to be in the 1860s and clearly shows the paucity of the first railway terminus in the town. A horse omnibus from the George Hotel awaits custom.

Osterfield Collection

branch was not of any great duration for No. 1 went to Rhymney in 1847 whilst No. 2 retired to a highly sedentary role in 1855, heating footwarmers at the Birmingham New Street station of the LNWR.

On 15th January 1840 the Aylesbury Railway was leased to the L&B for five years. After six months it must have been quite heartening for the promoters to see their confidence rewarded as the published passenger receipts of 30th December totalled 20,120 since the line's opening; they had paid £7,455 with not a single mishap on the branch itself. Such a success was the new railway that a public meeting held in the town hall was emphatic and unanimous to petition the Postmaster General to speed the mails by having them delivered to the town by railway.

Understandably the novelty had subsided somewhat nine months later in September 1841 when passenger figures were down to 16,301 with corresponding receipts of £6,042.

It was not however joy unconfined for everyone, as the railway came into conflict with old country ways that were not attuned so readily to the effects of its arrival. A locomotive was nearly derailed in collision with Mr Cook's cows of Wingrave. His application for compensation of £45 was not in this heady age received with consideration. Although criticism of him allowing the cows to stray on the line was valid, it would also, one would have thought, be an appropriate moment to focus attention on the cavalier attitude of early locomotive engineers with regard to brakes which were more implied rather than effective.

Another familiar casualty of the old ways was the local stage coaches. Their distances were being outpaced as they tried to maintain services by working with the railway. For example the Banbury to London coach now connected with the train at Aylesbury 'up' one day and 'down' the next. But the situation in such rural areas as north Bucks and Oxfordshire was that as the railways extended coach working became uneconomical and any towns or villages that had a through coach service suddenly found themselves cut-off until the nearest railhead could be built.

As the 1840s continued there was a gradually increased awakening to the potential of railways, influential people that had been effective opponents, especially in the landed classes, began to realise that they could turn them to advantage with the burgeoning demands in towns and cities for the supply of produce from their estates. The success of the Aylesbury Railway added further to this momentum that increased to hurricane force, with proposals for new lines flying around parliamentary chambers like a paper maelstrom. Parliament had never been deluged with anything like it before, committees had to be formed to make preliminary examinations of the validity of many conflicting schemes whilst there was some attempt to stall the further confusion of proliferating gauge choices. This was manifest by the appointment of a Royal Commission on gauges on 25th June 1845. Evidence of the force of this speculative deluge can be gained by the fact that 272 schemes received the Act of Royal Assent in 1846. Proportionately one can assume that a greater abundance of chaff was thrown out!

This preamble is intended to place into contemporary understanding the climate of ideas and proposals for lines affecting the Aylesbury Railway, which, but for the failure of Medley's Bank at Aylesbury, which caused an uncomfortable financial hiatus in the district, may well have been proceeded with to Oxford in 1839. That being the case the first Oxford station could have occurred in 1840, four years before the Great Western Railway got there! However, the plan was not to fail only once. In 1840 there was talk in Aylesbury of continuing the line to Thame and Oxford. The 1845 scheme for a railway from Tring to Aylesbury, with a branch to Thame via the Cuddington Valley (10 miles), continued through Bicester, Banbury, Evesham, Worcester and Wolverhampton. It is interesting as it took in Aylesbury in its belligerent attempt to defeat two broad gauge proposals supported by the Great Western Railway, the Oxford & Rugby and the Oxford, Worcester & Wolverhampton. The London & Birmingham's London, Worcester & South Staffordshire Railway was the result of some capricious railway politics of the day across this territory with the original Stephenson gauge 4ft 8½ins, disparagingly called the 'coal cart' gauge by the refined vision of Brunel's railway of 7ft 0¼in. It was not surprising that such maulings should inevitably wound both parties. The broad gauge schemes succeeded but had to concede in the Act to a statutory clause for inserting a third rail within their gauge to make the 'coal cart' gauge possible for any connections that may be required. Not the unqualified victory the broad gauge needed.

The untiring energy of railway speculation continued unabated throughout the 1840s with the Aylesbury Railway on several occasions being drawn into some protracted scheme or another. The Midland Grand Junction Railway 1845, was a company with an imposing title and a lofty ideal but out of its depth. Sandwiched between the two large companies it proposed to build a line from Reading, presumably with the acquiescence of the GWR to Henley, Marlow, High Wycombe, Princes Risborough, Aylesbury, Bucking-

ham, Blisworth and Northampton. For obvious reasons (their own proposals) the L&B opposed it most vigorously and it was eclipsed.

From the outset the people of Aylesbury had wanted a connection with Oxford which brought about a number of meetings in the town to discuss two rival schemes for the route. On the 4th April 1845 a special meeting of the Aylesbury Railway was held in the White Hart, Aylesbury to consider the claims of the Cambridge to Oxford Railway and the Aylesbury to Thame Railway. A number of members of the board of the AR were also on the Board of the L&B which was in fact promoting, along with local interests, a separate line, or three separate companies to build a railway from Oxford to Cambridge; the Oxford to Bletchley, the Bedford Railway which was at that time being constructed, and with the Eastern Counties Railway a line from Bedford to Cambridge. It was therefore surprising to find them supporting the Cambridge to Oxford Railway and opposing the Aylesbury to Thame. The Cambridge to Oxford hoped to approach the line from the east and tunnel under the L&B main line to join the Aylesbury branch two furlongs from Cheddington station, also with a spur from their line running north alongside the L&B.

The Aylesbury and Thame would simply butt end-on to the AR in the town, and would presumably be the first stage of a line to Oxford.

The aforementioned support appears to have been promulgated with a certain amount of duplicity by the L&B board members who merely curried favour to kill off the A&T which they successfully did. That being done the C&O discovered the iron fist in the velvet glove and it was then their turn to be attacked and mauled to the point of reduction; the section between Royston and Hitchin. This left the Aylesbury Railway losing out twice which could not have endeared them much to the L&B. Even less when a London & Oxford Railway of 1845 revealed the true motives of the L&B proposing their route to Uxbridge, High Wycombe, West Wycombe, Saunderton, Aston Rowant, with a branch to Thame (thus opposition to Aylesbury & Thame) through Cowley to Oxford. Another example of the protracted gauge conflict as the broad gauge had recently entered the outskirts of Oxford in 1844. However this was seen as an attempt to duplicate the GWR from London and was successfully fought off by them. Thereby the L&B had stifled schemes suitable to the Aylesbury branch only to fail by its own measure, leaving nothing.

By 1845 with extensions of adjoining railways on the L&B to York and Lancaster, the main line was having to handle 16 trains from Euston on weekdays between 6.15am and 9.00pm. This included two Aylesbury trains, two for Wolverton and one for Tring which was the section described as local service. This brought the L&B a dividend of 10% on passenger miles making them reluctant to interpose goods workings.

The White Hart Hotel, Aylesbury where so many meetings concerning railways were held. The Aylesbury Railway itself took form in the thoughts of its promoters within its walls. It was demolished in the 1860s.

Osterfield Collection

As previously mentioned, the formation and purchase of the Aylesbury line by the LNWR in 1846 left the possibilities of any extension totally under their control. Oddly a few months later the LNWR proposed a scheme that totally ignored the branch but if it had been successful would have decimated its London traffic – the London, Oxford & Cheltenham Railway. Once more the focus was on the developing spa town. This followed similar to the 1836 scheme with the junction at Tring passing through Aylesbury and branching a line to Oxford just north of that city. What the LNWR proposed to do about their recent purchase, the Aylesbury branch, if this scheme was successful is not clear. However it was not and the situation did not arise.

Unswerved by the failure of the LO&C railway, the LNWR found useful support in the area for a Buckinghamshire Railway plan. This was the extension of rail connection across the area supported by Sir Harry Verney of Claydon House who had supported the building of the Aylesbury Railway and the Duke of Buckingham of Stowe whose grandfather had so vehemently opposed the early survey of the main line of the L&B. A not exceptional twist of family viewpoint that brought the present Duke to the heights of Chairman of the LNWR from 1853 – 1861. The plan enjoined by the local luminaries and the directors of the LNWR was to extended a branch from Bletchley to Oxford, east to west with another line dissecting it south to north, Aylesbury to Brackley, carried beyond to Banbury solely at the wishes of the LNWR who hoped to cut off the GWR business with a West Midland route

to Birmingham. The weakest factor in the otherwise amicable arrangement between the Oxford to Bletchley Railway and the Buckingham & Brackley Junction Railway, that later formed the Buckinghamshire Railway, was the southern arm to Aylesbury. The LNWR could see little point in this but grudgingly accepted it, whilst the local interest saw it as the attainment of a local ideal, to have Aylesbury on a through route with connections not only south but north, plus the east-west link. Unfortunately for Aylesbury, which would have prospered as a result of such an early important connection, the LNWR's reluctance was aided by a financial panic in 1847, before the Aylesbury line was started and so were able to lever, that to have their continuing support for the other two schemes, which were now under construction, the Aylesbury line must be dropped. Thus the original Aylesbury line that had not for the first time seemed in prospect of greater things, remained like an unrequited stump, always on the point of budding and bursting forth into other directions.

After the opening of the entire Buckinghamshire Railway system by 1851 another attempt was made by the LNWR to revive their Tring, Oxford Railway in 1853 which became ludicrously cut down to a connecting spur between the LNWR and GWR at Yarnton near Oxford. This railway had the misfortune to get through the House of Commons to be thrown back by the House of Lords. It proposed to leave the LNWR main line at Tring and join the Aylesbury Railway at the 3 milepost, the place close by where later the Marston

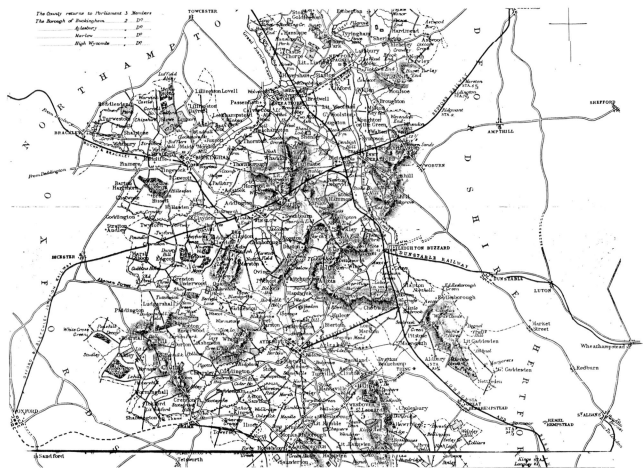

The surveys of 1845 showing the Oxford and Bletchley line and eventual branch to Banbury. The southern arm to Aylesbury was not built.

Andrew Emmerson

Gate station would be built, at Marston Crossing. Using the Aylesbury line it continued to Haddenham, Thame, Holton and north of Oxford at Yarnton, presumably to join with the OW&WR there. It appears that there was much opposition in the town of Aylesbury to this line crossing the High Street on the level.

A meeting of another Aylesbury & Thame Railway took place at the Spread Eagle Hotel, Thame in 1860. Not to connect this time with the Aylesbury Railway, they had probably had enough of that one, but to connect with the newly proposed Aylesbury & Buckingham Railway to Verney Junction. This scheme seems to have found itself snagged in a thicket of conflicting proposals as the Wycombe Railway was planning a line from Princes Risborough to Aylesbury and another to Thame. With the backing of the GWR it was able to draw on capital interest in this area and starve out the other concern. In the final shape of lines the Thame and Aylesbury never did have a direct rail connection as this could only be achieved by changing at Prince Risborough. Probably the last attempt to extend the Aylesbury branch and the one that came closest to succeeding, was the Aylesbury & Buckingham Railway scheme of

1861. This was in effect a revival of the unfulfilled cruciform of the Buckinghamshire Railway days, the branch south to Aylesbury connecting up with the existing line.

The failure of the link at Aylesbury was in part due to a local difference on land purchasing and the lukewarm persuasion of the chairman of the LNWR.

Although in 1863 the town was by no means as built up as it is today there were nevertheless a number of buildings in the path of the connection and most of these were satisfactorily purchased under the Act of the A&B.

Between the stations was to be an extension empowered by the LNWR from their station directly through a hostelry called the Bear Inn, the proprietor of which was holding out for more agreeable compensation. This was in fact the last property outstanding. The asking price of the proprietor was £2,950 for the inn and £500 for the gardens adjoining. The LNWR offered £395 and the matter was submitted to jurisprudence.

However it appears that the chairman of the LNWR had little patience with a long saga of litigation and after meeting deputations of the A&B in May and July of 1866, which in view of the situation was probably a plaintiff appeal by them, he instructed the LNWR solicitor to withdraw. This left the Aylesbury & Buckingham with a railway of five years in the making, for only twelve miles and no agreement with the larger company for hire of locomotives and stock.

As already described the LNWR had not been particularly encouraging with regard to the connecting link north of Aylesbury in 1847. This new undertaking had formerly had the support of the Marquess of Chandos when chairman of the LNWR and of the A&B at a meeting on 9th June 1861. By 1861 he had left the company to become President of Madras and had no further connection with it. Richard Moon, the new chairman of the LNWR, probably felt he could dispassionately uphold the feelings of 1847. It has to be admitted that it is difficult to see of what possible benefit this loop via Aylesbury could be alongside the established line via Bletchley. He would also have much more to consider in the erstwhile herculean prospect of the quadrupling of the main line that was now in prospect.

The Aylesbury & Buckingham was built and opened but at a crippling and unremunerative expense to its promoters it became dependent on the GWR's Wycombe Railway for loan of locomotives and stock.

The Wycombe Railway brought the broad gauge from Princes Risborough into Aylesbury on 1st October 1863. It was the furthest eastern probe of the famous 7ft. Conversion to standard gauge of this line took place on 21st October 1868, after the Wycombe Railway had been merged into the GWR proper. The conversion would allow through working at a joint station with the A&B at Aylesbury which is the way things remained for 25 years.

In terms of the LNWR branch to Aylesbury, competition had now arrived with the new station which encouraged passengers and trade to prefer the London terminus of Paddington and all the stations en route.

On 5th September 1863 the local press reported the progress of the competing line. ". . . the old buildings in the Oxford Road have been removed and the road is now open from the new railway station to The Bell corner. For some reason of which it is not known the opening of the line has been deferred but we understand that it is contemplated to run five trains daily 'up' and 'down', the fares to be the same as those on the North Western. The journey to London to be accomplished in one hour and three quarters. Competitively the LNWR are running more trains between Aylesbury and London with no less than ten trains daily. Some of the trains have also been accelerated within eighty minutes of each other. A person can now leave Aylesbury in time to breakfast in London, return to Aylesbury for luncheon and go back to London to dine, return again to Aylesbury to tea, go once more to London to supper and be home to Aylesbury to take a pipe." Hopefully a none too dyspeptic day of journeys!

With regard to competition, the GWR arrival was but a side show to what was over the horizon both north and south. By 1894 in a series of masterly strokes by its chairman, Sir Edward Watkin, the young Metropolitan Railway drove north up the Missenden Valley and finally reached Aylesbury and absorbed the A&B to Verney Junction. In its wake it seeded the new commuter land and gave Aylesbury the boost it needed – direct rail service over 40 miles into the new terminus of Baker Street with its developing Metropolitan connection. This firmly circumscribed the once important branch of the Aylesbury Railway. The short comings of connections at remote Cheddington was hardly likely to retain attraction against the new modus operandi of fast arterial connection to the Capital. What remained in business north of Cheddington was soon to be similarly drawn away to more attractive connections in the ensuing five years.

Sir Edward Watkin had hoped to draw the Metropolitan further north with greater ambitions. This was the breathtaking vision of a trunk line from the industrial north to south, crossing London and by means of another of his companies, the South Eastern & Chatham to reach the south coast and a Channel tunnel beneath that embattled moat of water, the English Channel. The unrealised transcontinental route was not all that foundered, for the Metropolitan Railway was not much in favour of extending its capital undertaking further from the Metropolis than rural Bucks and the plans for commuter expansion. Having reached this limitation it was then a matter of arousing the ambitions of a northern railway under his chairmanship, the Manchester, Sheffield & Lincolnshire. An extension to London from Annesly, linking with the Metropolitan at Quainton just north of Aylesbury a distance of nearly 92 miles appeared a logical step and so in 1893 the scheme received the Royal Assent.

What all this has to do with the Aylesbury branch of the LNWR must appear fairly obvious, for with the opening of this new railway called the Great Central in 1899, there was a fast main line service north as well as south of Aylesbury. With the enlargement and rebuilding of the Met. & GCR station in the town, the prime mover of the town's transport business cannot be denied. It is fair to say that the LNWR had not been complacent since the opening of the original station as a new and better facilitated station had been opened by them for the branch on ground on the southern side of the gasworks in 1889. But in the face of such strong competition in the years that followed it has to be admitted that the days of its greater glory had well and truly passed. As the remainder of the book will reveal, the line remained useful for some passengers seeking, for one reason or another, to use the West Coast Main Line, by a large proportion, to go north, plus a smaller number as a local service. However, goods traffic did remain substantial into the 1960s. Historically its outstanding claim remained with that early heroic age when it was kindred to the building of the London & Birmingham Railway.

Chapter 2

The Line

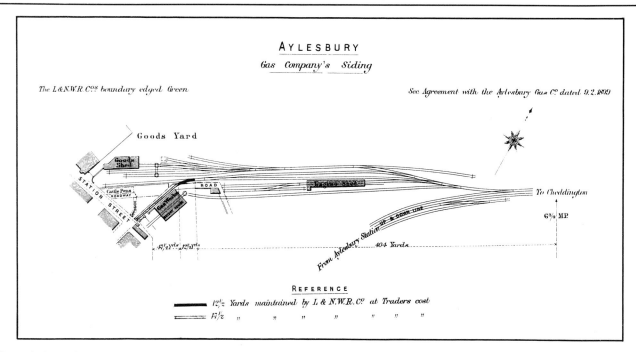

Ground plans of the goods yard area from the LNWR book of private sidings dated January 1901. This refers to the installation of the gasworks siding alongside the retort house. Note the cattle pens are built on the original 'down' platform of the original station.
John Pritchett Collection

Comparison between the track diagrams of the first Aylesbury station on Station Street and the second on the High Street will reveal two stations of quite separate periods of railway development. The paucity of the former reflects the early railway age when, due to the restraint of cost, termini were held moribund within small land areas. With increasing trade more sidings were added and boundaries expanded until a modest terminus like Aylesbury covered a considerable percentage of the town centre land area.

The platform of the first station is much shorter, as were the trains of four-wheel coaches, similar to stagecoaches and pulled by small engines. The method of handling stock is evident from the diagram, with turntables and end-loading docks suggesting the muscle power of man and horse. Clearance around the tables would be to allow space to manoeuvre. This station is appropriately of modest dimensions, partitioned into small cramped rooms to which, shortly after opening, was added a glazed canopy covering one set of rails. Clearly with so little accommodation much of the populace would spend their time standing on that platform.

The goods shed seems absurdly sited, almost blocking the entrance to the yard. It will be noted on the later plan that the LNWR simply cut one corner off to gain greater clearance.

Much has been written on early signalling, or the shortcomings of it and apart from the serious risk of annihilating Her Majesty's subjects, if the results of a

mere branch off the main line is anything to go by, greater control would recover, if nothing else, the cost of smashed crossing-gates!

A half-yearly report of the Aylesbury Railway for 16th March 1843 states that cottages have been erected at crossings Dropshort (Park Street), Broughton and Long Marston where policemen are occupied for duty. Like the main line the control of trains would be on the time interval and hand semaphore system. With constables positioned one mile apart with red and white flags and lamp for night duty to show white – line clear, green – slow down, red – stop. Constables were at crossings only on the branch and worked as gatemen. In this pre-lock and block age all point switches would be in the open and operated by a switchman.

Following the line through to Cheddington the trains would reach the first level crossing at Dropshort, where, after a grisly accident in 1883 a footbridge was added over the line. Up until then the constable or 'bobby' would have the job of ensuring that the company's business proceeded effectively, including the safety of the local population. As well as operating the rudimentary signalling installed to protect the gates, he needed to ensure that drivers knew that they were coming to the end of the line.

All of this became much more effectively served with the building of a signal box of type 4 LNWR pattern c1889. After absolute 'block' had been brought in on the branch on 18th November 1880 the control of traffic at the station was administered by operation of the box 32

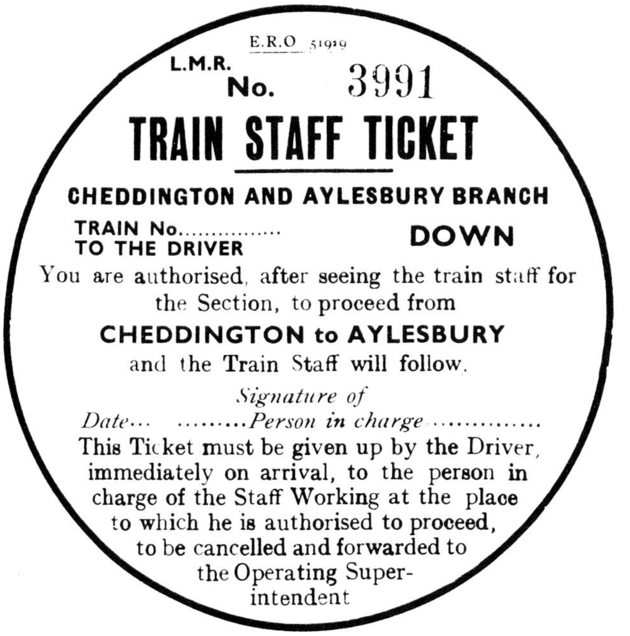
E.R.O 51919
L.M.R.
No. 3991
TRAIN STAFF TICKET
CHEDDINGTON AND AYLESBURY BRANCH
TRAIN No...............
TO THE DRIVER
DOWN
You are authorised, after seeing the train staff for the Section, to proceed from
CHEDDINGTON to AYLESBURY
and the Train Staff will follow.
Signature of
Date··· ·········*Person in charge*·············
This Ticket must be given up by the Driver, immediately on arrival, to the person in charge of the Staff Working at the place to which he is authorised to proceed, to be cancelled and forwarded to the Operating Superintendent

Train Staff Ticket for 'down' trains to be surrendered to the signalman at Aylesbury. *Len Kinchen's Collection*

lever frame, one of which released the additional ground frame at the station.

There were only two continuing block posts on the branch, Aylesbury and Cheddington. Marston Crossing was switched in at certain peak times.

Access to the line was by train staff and ticket, tickets issued from the staff station with the last in that direction taking the staff itself, prohibiting further departures from that station until it had returned. Most of the time there was only one engine using the line which usually meant that it simply carried the staff up and down the line.

After Dropshort is the area known as Stocklake, about the 6½ milepost. On one side was the Aylesbury Gaol, which became for part of its existence, a womens' prison and during that time held the notorious poisoner Mrs Lawrence Maybrick. As a result of this railway men called the siding alongside the running line here 'Mrs Maybrick's siding'.

In the flat open farming country that follows are the nearby villages of Bierton and Burcott, the road between them and the village of Broughton – Burcott Lane, was the site of another crossing and cottage, with a hut for signalling equipment on the opposite side of the road. This held the block repeater indicator which would show when a train was on the line. As there was no block bell the only means of being sure of an oncoming train was to check the indicator at the appropriate time. The fallibility of this system was little improved from the situation in the 1840s (time interval) and Broughton Crossing gates suffered often as a consequence. An attempt to ensure vigilance at the crossing was made with instructions for the keeper to ring Aylesbury box at 6am each morning to notify them he was on duty. This was a supplementary rule for block posts in the Working Appendix. At the end of the day, after the last scheduled train had gone by, the rule was to ring Aylesbury box to ask if there would be any more trains that day, who would know also from the Cheddington end. In the event of there being no more trains the keeper would then be able to sign off duty. Procedure in cases of emergency required a degree of athleticism, the keeper was liable to run with all speed in the direction of any oncoming train and place three detonators on the track before it reached the spot.

Attentiveness from both driver and crossing keeper needed to be sharpened to a keen edge in those early railway days when safety relied entirely on observation. On the evening of 3rd July 1849 the crossing keeper at Broughton received a startling and unscheduled train. This was the luggage train that had somehow managed to make off alone from the station and smashed through his crossing gates. Although another engine pursued it, it was not caught until it had exhausted its steam supply at Leighton! It is interesting to ruminate how it managed to get through the junction at Cheddington. Presumably no other train was in the vicinity or the consequences of unauthorised entry of the main line could have been

Passenger Timetable from Bradshaw's in 1909. *Author's Collection*

56	571 Redditch ...... arr.	7 33	8 32	1128	....	....	3 3	....	6 42	....	1022	....	....
52½	571 Evesham ...... "	7 33	8 28	1118	....	....	2 51	....	6 28	....	8 53	....	....
70¾	573 Cheltenham †. "	....	9 27	1213	....	....	4 0	....	7 56	....	....	....	....

	404 Rugby .... "	....	1115	....	....	....	[illegible] 40	....	....	7 15	....	1047c	
171½	405 Manchester § .. "	....	2 27	....	....	....	6 5	....	....	1035	....	2c58	....
62	413 Bletchley ..... "	....	1052	....	....	....	2 16	....	....	6c46	....	9c50	....
108¾	413 London (Euston) "	....	12 0	....	....	....	4 5	....	....	8c25	....	1125c	

a Through Carriage to London (Marylebone).
b By Through Slip Carriage to Stratford-on-Avon.
c Via Northampton.
h Through Carriage to Stratford-on-Avon.
m By Slip Carriage.
n Arrives at 1 40 on Sunday mornings.
t Tuesdays only.
* Woodford and Hinton.
† S. M. J. Station, 1 mile from G. W. Station.
‡ Queen's Road, Lansdown.
§ London Road.

For OTHER TRAINS between Blisworth and Towcester, see page 441.

LONDON, CHEDDINGTON, and AYLESBURY.—London and North Western. [London and Aylesbury.

Miles.	Down.	Week Days.											Sundays.	
		mrn	mrn	mrn	mrn	aft	aft	aft	aft	aft	aft	aft	mrn	aft
	404 London (Euston) ...... dep.	6 10	7 45	9 10	11 5	1220	1 45	3 0	5 0	6 10	7 10	....	9 0	2 45
	413 Leighton .... "	7 8	8 26	10 3	1222	....	2 42	4 33	....	7 2	7 45	9 17	7 42	4 30
—	Cheddington .... dep.	7 40	8 45	1040	1240	1 40	3 15	4 48	6 0	7 20	8 35	9 30	1025	4 40
2¾	Marston Gate	7 47	8 52	1047	1247	1 47	3 22	4 55	6 7	7 27	8 42	9 37	1032	4 47
7	Aylesbury ‖ 411, 396 ... arr.	7 57	9 0	1055	1255	1 57	3 30	5 3	6 15	7 35	8 50	9 48	1042	4 57

Miles	Up.	Week Days.												Sundays.		
		mrn	mrn	mrn	non	aft	aft	aft Except Weds.	aft Weds. only.	aft	aft	aft	aft	mrn	mrn	aft
	Aylesbury .... dep.	7 5	8 12	9 10	12 0	1 10	2 15	3 55	4 0	5 30	6 30	8 0	9 0	7 25	10 0	5 5
4¼	Marston Gate	7 15	8 21	9 19	12 9	1 19	2 26	4 4	4 9	5 39	6 39	8 9	9 9	7 35	10 9	5 15
7	Cheddington 404, 413 ... arr.	7 22	8 30	9 25	1215	1 26	2 33	4 10	4 15	5 45	6 45	8 15	9 15	7 42	1015	5 22
11¼	404 Leighton .... arr.	7 40	8 57	9 40	1233	1 44	3 20	4 27	4 27	6 3	7 0	8 35		....	1030	5 33
43	413 London (Euston) ..... "	8 45	9 35	1025	1 50	3s50	4 5	6 5	6 5	....	8 25	....	1025	9 25	1245	7 40

s Saturdays only. ‖ High Street; nearly 1 mile to the G. W. Station.

NOTE.—The Level Crossing Gates are closed against the Line each night from after the passage of the last Booked Train to 7.0 a.m. Any train running over the Branch between these hours must stop for the Fireman or Breaksman to open and close the Gates, unless special arrangements have been made beforehand for the Gates to be open.

AYLESBURY BRANCH—SINGLE LINE. Train Staff Stations—CHEDDINGTON and AYLESBURY.

Distance from Chedd'gton	DOWN WEEK DAYS.	1	2	3	4	5	6	7	8	9
			Goods	Mixed Train	Pass	Pass		Pass		Pass
			M							
Miles.			a.m.	a m	a m	a m		p.m.		p.m.
...	Cheddington ... ... dep.	...	6 0	7 40	8 45	10 40	...	12 40	...	1 40
2 3/8	Marston Gate ... ... ,,	...	X	7 47	8 52	10 47	...	12 47	...	1 47
6 7/8	AYLESBURY ... arr.	...	6 25	7 57	9 0	10 55	...	12 55	...	1 57

Distance from Chedd'gton	DOWN WEEK DAYS.	10	11	12	13	14	15	16	17
		Coal.	Pass	Pass	Pass	C Eng. and Break.	Pass	Pass	Mixed Train
						W O			
Miles.		p m	p m	p.m.	p.m.	p.m.	p m	p.m.	p.m.
...	Cheddington ... ... dep.	2 40	3 15	4 48	6 0	6 12	7 20	8 35	9 30
2 3/8	Marston Gate ... ... ,,	3E0	3 22	4 55	6 7	...	7 27	8 42	9 37
6 7/8	AYLESBURY ... arr.	3 10	3 30	5 3	6 15	6 29	7 35	8 50	9 48

Distance from Chedd'gton	DOWN SUNDAYS.	18	19	20	21	22	23
			Cattle and Goods.	Pass		Pass	Light Eng.
							C
Miles.			a m	a m		p m	p.m.
...	Cheddington ... ... dep.	...	8 5	10 25	See note.	4 40	9 55
2 3/8	Marston Gate ... ... ,,	...	8 14	10 32		4 47	...
6 7/8	AYLESBURY ... arr.	...	8 24	10 42		4 57	10 15

Distance from Ay'esbury	UP WEEK DAYS	24	25	26	27	28	29	30	31	32
		Eng. & Brk.	Pass	Mixed Train	Pass	Pass	Pass	Mixed Train	Pass	Mixed Train
		M		S	S O		S	S O		
Miles.		a.m.	a m	a m	a.m.	a m	noon	noon	p.m.	p m
...	AYLESBURY ... dep.	4 35	7 5	8 12	8 12	9 10	12 0	12 0	1 10	2 15
4 1/4	Marston Gate ... ... ,,	...	7 15	8 23	8 21	9 19	12 9	12 11	1 19	2 26
6 7/8	Cheddington .. ... arr.	4 55	7 22	8 30	8 27	9 25	12 15	12 18	1 26	2 33

Distance from Ay'esbury	UP WEEK DAYS	33	34	35	36	37	38	39	40
		Pass	Pass	Pass	C Cattle	Pass	Goods	Pass	Pass
		W	W O		W O				
Miles.		p.m.	p.m.	p.m.	p.m.	p m	p m	p.m.	p.m.
...	AYLESBURY ... dep.	3 55	4 0	5 30	5 40	6 30	7 40	8 0	9 0
4 1/4	Marston Gate ... ... ,,	4 4	4 9	5 39	...	6 39	X	8 9	9 9
6 7/8	Cheddington .. ... arr.	4 10	4 15	5 45	5 55	6 45	7 55	8 15	9 15

Distance from Ay'esbury	UP SUNDAYS.	41	42	43	44	45	46
		Pass		Pass		Pass	Cattle
							C
Miles.		a m		a m		p m	p.m.
...	AYLESBURY ... dep.	7 25	...	10 0	See note.	5 5	10 30
4 1/4	Marston Gate ... ... ,,	7 35	...	10 9		5 15	...
6 7/8	Cheddington .. ... arr.	7 42	...	10 15		5 22	10 50

E No. 10 Down, 12.30 p.m. from Bletchley, arrive Marston Gate 2.50 p.m. No. 22 is 4.30 p.m. from Leighton. No. 38 runs to Bletchley. No. 45 runs to Leighton.

Working Timetable for 1902. Most trains were hauled by the same engine until the 2.40pm 'down' coal which required an extra engine in the diagram, which would bring in 'ticket' working. Wednesday only trains were by reason of that being market day in Aylesbury. Note the cattle train working on a Sunday.

P.R.H. Webber Collection

In 1921 the ramifications of the war and increasing road competition had taken their toll. Sunday trains were ended even in the working timetable in the Second World War. It is interesting that there was no 'down' goods, being designated 'mixed', but a return working is designated 'goods' – No. 46, presumably the 'down' mineral would bring the return goods working.

John Lowe Collection

NOTE.—The Level Crossing Gates are closed against the Line each week night from after the passage of the last Booked Train to 6.35 a.m., and from after the passage of the last booked train on Saturday to 6.35 a.m. Monday. Any train running over the Branch between these hours must stop for the Fireman or Goods Guard to open and close the Gates, unless special arrangements have been made beforehand for the Gates to be open.

AYLESBURY BRANCH—SINGLE LINE. Train Staff Stations—CHEDDINGTON and AYLESBURY.

Distance from Chedd'gton	DOWN. WEEK DAYS ONLY.	1	2	3	4	5	6	7	8	9	10	11	12
					Mixed		Pass.			Pass.	Pass.	Pass.	Pass
												S	S O
Miles.					a m		a m			a.m.	p.m.	p.m.	p.m.
...	Cheddington ... ... dep.	...	...	...	7 25	...	8 59	...	...	10 35	12 38	1 40	2 5
2 1/4	Marston Gate ... ,,	...	...	...	7 33	...	9 6	...	...	10 42	12 45	1 47	2 12
6 7/8	AYLESBURY ... arr.	...	...	...	7 44	...	9 16	...	...	10 52	12 55	1 57	2 22

Distance from Chedd'gton	DOWN. WEEK DAYS ONLY.	13	14	15	16	17	18	19	20	21	22	23
		Mineral	Pass.		Pass.		Pass.		Pass.		Mixed	
Miles.		p m	p.m.		p.m.		p.m.		p.m.		p.m.	
...	Cheddington ... ... dep.	3 5	3 40	...	5 8	...	6 10	...	7 35	...	8 50	...
2 1/4	Marston Gate ... ,,	E	3 47	...	5 15	...	6 17	...	7 42	...	8 58	...
6 7/8	AYLESBURY ... arr.	3 30	3 57	...	5 25	...	6 27	...	7 52	...	9 9	...

Distance from Aylesbury	UP. WEEK DAYS ONLY	25	26	27	28	29	30	31	32	33	34	35	36
				Pass.		Pass.		Pass.		Mixed			
Miles.				a m	...	a.m.		a m		a.m.			
...	AYLESBURY ... dep.	...	...	6 30	...	8 5	...	9 30	...	11 45	...	...	...
4 1/4	Marston Gate ... ... ,,	...	...	6 41	...	8 16	...	9 41	...	11 57	...	...	...
6 7/8	Cheddington ... ... arr.	...	...	6 47	...	8 22	...	9 47	...	12 4	...	...	...

Distance from Aylesbury	UP. WEEK DAYS ONLY	37	38	39	40	41	42	43	44	45	46	47
		Mixed		Pass.	Pass.		Pass.			Pass.	Goods	Pass.
Miles.		p.m.		p.m.	p.m.		p.m.			p.m.	p.m.	p.m.
...	AYLESBURY ... dep.	1 5	...	2 40	4 20	...	5 40	...	...	6 40	6 55	8 5
4 1/4	Marston Gate ... ... ,,	1 17	...	2 51	4 31	...	5 51	...	...	6 51	7 18	8 16
6 7/8	Cheddington ... ... arr.	1 24	...	2 57	4 37	...	5 57	...	...	6 57	7 28	8 22

E No. 13 Down, 1.30 p.m. from Bletchley, No. 46 runs to Bletchley. Calls at Marston Gate Tuesdays, Thursdays, and Saturdays only, arrive 7.10 p.m.

AYLESBURY AND NEWPOR

grave indeed. Another example, on 24th June 1861 the 7am train from Aylesbury smashed straight through the Broughton Road crossing carrying both gates away on its buffer beam. In the event the injured party was the company that had to pay to replace them, with no doubt some serious words for the crossing keeper that had overslept. As the tiny crossing house is beside the crossing such a pandemonium would have brought his slumbers to an abrupt finale.

It is fair to say a feature of the Aylesbury branch is that it is featureless in terms of its engineering. Few lines could have been easier to build with no gradients of note. Some gradient boards were in four figures! To illustrate just how little the route was affected by the terrain, one engineman described that whilst running on the branch and leaving the curve at Cheddington they could see from one end to the other. Starting from Cheddington at night the lights of Aylesbury never veered from just over the smokebox end.

Marston Crossing and the keeper's house would not have been so isolated had Robert Stephenson's first survey been left unrevised. For this survey placed the railway close to the northern edge of the village. In the event it was redrawn nearly a mile further away placing it approximately half way between Marston and Wingrave. Its first use as a station was as early as 1857 but it was some seven years later that the installations were built to recognise it as a station proper and included in local timetables.

Most of Marston Gate's goods traffic was milk, cattle and manure besides the multifarious needs of farming communities, this being the reason for a station being there first of all. Inevitably such isolated railheads would feel the first effects of mechanisation, more extensively after the First World War, when milk collection became concentrated in centralised road depots. Whilst cattle traffic was consistent until specialised road vehicles became more effective after the Second World War, it appears that Marston Gate was in decline from the late 1930s.

Soon after Marston Gate the line comes within sight of Mentmore with the house across the fields set in its woodlands like some imperial palace. The Rosebery's like the Rothschilds before them would scarce afford a glance at the branch line railway to Aylesbury that impertinently dissects the fringes of their estate, though they may often have had to wait in their gleaming crest emblazoned carriages at the crossing. The right of procession being with the railway that was hauling its trains long before Mentmore had been hewn from its stone.

The crossing was situated on the southern driveway to the house and remained as a piece of railway antiquity when at one time it seemed more likely in 1867 that it would be dispensed with and replaced with a bridge, and plans were drawn up.

With the building and staffing of the house it would become necessary to have this crossing manned as it had not been hitherto. Guests attending weekend functions would be arriving and leaving for many hours which required the crossing to be manned for excessively long periods. The company contractor was approached, Mr Woodham, who recommended first of all a cottage for the 'bobby', or a bridge, doing away with the crossing altogether which would cost £1,000. Further, Baron Rothschild offered land and £200 towards the construction of it. In the light of this it is remarkable that the plan was not carried through. What did transpire was that the crossing was manned in two shifts with the men living in the village and retaining a hut with repeating block indicator instrument to inform trains on the line, hand lamps, flags and detonators. Later a telephone was added while in early days there had been a signal post on the 'down' side, before the gates.

Like Aylesbury, Cheddington has two distinct periods, the first as a small station for interchange with the main line and the branch. The illustration in this book will show how meagre this was even after some elaboration from its first years. The main buildings were on the 'down' side with a second island platform on the 'up', its outer face accommodating the relief line for southbound trains between Bletchley and Willesden. The second era, after quadrupling, involved a marginal resiting of the station as well as extensive rebuilding with realignment of the branch platform with four faces for the main line connected by a 42ft 9in footbridge.

This completed the journey of seven miles that had so often been in prospect of going further. Particularly the 1846 connection of the Buckinghamshire Railway, for with the success of that the line would have been part of a cross-country route that would have connected with the GWR at Banbury, but which never occurred directly. Aylesbury would have had a central expanding station to be connected eventually with the GWR from Princes Risborough, the Metropolitan from the south and the Great Central Railway from the north, possibly using LNWR metals from Claydon Junction.

Bradshaw's in 1942 with six 'down' trains and six 'up', the most meagre service since 1839 that was improved before closure in 1953.
Author's Collection

Chapter 3

Aylesbury

Aylesbury station in LNWR vintage, though probably during the 1920s. Clearly, traffic is brisk with the horse vans in the appropriate loading dock and a train in the station platform road. Note the nameboard for 'Aylesbury' right, believed to be white letters on blue or black ground surrounded by a white moulded frame.

L&GRP Courtesy of David & Charles

In the burgeoning industrial heartlands of the 19th century it had been canals that had first set the pace of transport expansion. This was a vigorous system that preceded the dawn of the railway era with its own pioneers and industrial folklore. The Grand Junction Canal sought a shorter route to Birmingham than by Oxford and was completed in 1805, the year after Richard Trevithick first steamed his engine at Penydarren Ironworks, Merthyr Tydfil. The success of the Grand Junction Canal had a drastic effect along its length with sleepy cottage industries suddenly being eclipsed by the mass transportation of cheaper bricks, pottery and china whilst the arrival of coal in quantities was a positive impetus to others like the gas industry.

Both north Bucks towns of Buckingham and Aylesbury had branches from this canal. The Aylesbury branch was opened in 1815, a 6 1/4 mile route from the main water at Marsworth. Ironically the branch predated the same frustrations as the railway, having reached the town it had difficulties in finding extension further which had been the plan at the outset. It was to connect with a projected Thames & Wilts & Berks Canal at Abingdon which in fact was never cut. Consequently the Aylesbury branch, though a boon to the town was seen as dead water to the Board of the Grand Junction.

Nevertheless, unlike the Buckingham branch it prospered and continued to do so long after the railways were established in the town, which says quite a lot for the commerce of the locality. It did eventually suffer a period of decline and dereliction but not beyond recovery, for today it is sufficiently bouyant to support the new role as a leisure waterway.

During the period of its early prosperity it saw a high summer of dividends paying 12% which would have been a positive eldorado to any subsequent railway company.

During the 1840s the canal did not entirely reflect prosperity, the rising birth rate and agricultural depressions blighted the local population of 5,000. Land enclosures in the countryside created the social iniquities of dispossession amongst the labouring classes and many people from the area were forced to consider emigration as a desperate solution. The canal wharves crowded with pathetic groups with expressions of bewilderment, anxiety and despair as they crowded into boats bound first of all to Liverpool and from there to the edge of the world for all they knew. This continued with a greater propensity with the opening of the railway.

Aylesbury Railway
IN CONJUNCTION WITH THE
LONDON AND BIRMINGHAM RAILWAY.

The Public are respectfully informed, that on and after Thursday, June 20th, 1839,

THE HOURS OF DEPARTURE will be as under :—
LONDON TO AYLESBURY.

8.0 A.M.	calling at all the Stations,	Due at CHEDDINGTON	9.45 A.M.
2.0 P.M.	ditto	ditto	3.45 P.M.
5.0 P.M.	ditto	ditto	6.45 P.M.

BIRMINGHAM TO AYLESBURY.

6.0 A.M.	calling at all the Stations,	Due at CHEDDINGTON	9.45 A.M.
3.30 P.M.	do. only at 1st Class ditto	ditto	6.55 P.M.

AYLESBURY TO LONDON.

7.10 A.M. joins 6¾ A.M. Train from WOLVERTON, Calling at all the Stations.
9.25 A.M. .. 6 A.M. ditto BIRMINGHAM, ditto.
6.25 P.M. .. 3¼ P.M. ditto Ditto Calling only at 1st Class ditto

AYLESBURY TO BIRMINGHAM.

9.25 A.M. joins 8 A.M. Train from LONDON, Calling at all the Stations.
3.25 P.M. .. 2 P.M. ditto . ditto.

On Sundays.
LONDON TO AYLESBURY.

8.0 A.M.	Calling at all the Stations,	Due at CHEDDINGTON	9.45 A.M.
5.0 P.M.	ditto	ditto	6.45 P.M.

BIRMINGHAM TO AYLESBURY.

1.30 P.M. Calling at all the Stations, Due at CHEDDINGTON 5.15 P.M.

AYLESBURY TO LONDON.

7.10 A.M. joins 6¾ A.M. Train from WOLVERTON, calling at all the Stations.
4.55 P.M. .. 1½ P.M. ditto BIRMINGHAM, ditto.

AYLESBURY TO BIRMINGHAM.

9.25 A.M. joins 8 A.M. Train from LONDON, calling at all the Stations.

Fares.

	First Class	Second Class
To or from AYLESBURY and LONDON	8s. 6d.	5s. 6d.
To or from AYLESBURY and BIRMINGHAM	21s. 6d.	14s. 6d.

Private Carriages and Horses must be at the Station at least 15 min. before the time of Departure.

The Company strongly recommend all Passengers to have their Name and Destination clearly stated on their Luggage, and to see that it is put upon the Carriages.

Parcels and Packages are carried by the Coach Trains and received at the various Offices as usual.
June, 1839.

HOWSON, PRINTER, 38, BARBICAN.

Arrangements to accommodate Aylesbury Railway trains by the London & Birmingham Railway. It appears that branch coaches were attached and detached to trains at Cheddington where there was possibly a locomotive stabling point to work the branch. The actual change station was probably Tring.
Aylesbury County Library

On 4th January 1842 a party of young men left Aylesbury railroad station early in the morning as emigrants to Sydney in New South Wales. They were from the neighbourhood of Risborough, they were all agricultural labourers.

One hundred and thirty left the Chinnor district for Port Phillip, Australia on the morning of 30th October

LONDON AND BIRMINGHAM RAILWAY.
COACHING DEPARTMENT.
HOURS OF DEPARTURE AND TIME TABLE.
(On and after Thursday, 20th June 1839)

DOWN TRAINS from LONDON.

UP TRAINS from BIRMINGHAM.

June, 1839.

HOWSON, Printer, Barbican.

Details of main line running in June 1839 when the Aylesbury Railway opened. The service had begun a year earlier with six trains each way taking 6 hours, by this time 5 and 5½ hours were achieved, over the distance of 116 miles. The 9.30am mails from Euston took 5 hours including stops at Tring (8 min.), Wolverton (10 min.), Weedon (3 min.) and Coventry (9 min.) making a total of 30 minutes without movement, allowing 4½ hours for the journey. The longer stoppages were for the Aylesbury branch mail at Tring and probably engine changing at Wolverton. All other trains had twelve vehicles or fifty wagons, while the 'mail' was restricted to six vehicles. Eight months after the introduction of this timetable two extra trains were introduced for the Aylesbury line, the 12 noon ex-Euston and the 4pm ex-Aylesbury.
Ron Miller Collection

1843. Seventy more left from the same district in December, with some desperation, to accept a hazardous sea voyage in the very depths of winter. Throughout the forties a steady stream departed from the district for Canada, USA and Australia. The relieving officer of the

local union workhouse organised groups of itinerant
poor. It was recorded that a number of paupers left the
establishment in March 1844 to be shipped overseas.
The fact that the railway provided transportation to
Liverpool, may have shortened the time of the journey,
that could have been little else but wretched, in view of
the conditions supplied by the railway for third class
passengers up until the introduction of 'Parliamentary'
trains.

Fortunately not all tasks were to prove so melancholy. In June 1842 the Aylesbury Railway advertised
an early rail excursion, a round trip to Gravesend at 8s
0d (40p) a head. Their enterprise was not ignored, for
300 passengers booked the trip which must have been as
exciting to them then as a journey to Australia would be
now. Some would certainly be seeing the sea for the first
time having spent their lives largely confined by parish
boundaries and the fields in which they worked. Further
the company began to issue cheap day returns at a third
less than the usual price in 1844.

Notice of opening of the line posted at Aylesbury, including
times of first trains.

Ron Miller Collection

AYLESBURY RAILWAY.

The Public are respectfully informed, that this Line of Railway

WILL BE OPENED

ON

MONDAY, 10 June 1839

For the conveyance of

PASSENGERS and PARCELS,

In conjunction with the

London and Birmingham Railway,

TO AND FROM

AYLESBURY AND LONDON.

Until further Notice, the following will be the
TIME OF DEPARTURE OF THE TRAINS.

UP - - Leaves *AYLESBURY* for LONDON,
Morning, 10m past **7**, half-past **10**. *Afternoon* 10 m past **6**.
On **SUNDAYS**, Morning 10 m. past 7. Afternoon, at 5.

DOWN - Leaves *LONDON* for AYLESBURY,
Morning, half-past **7**. *Afternoon*, **2** and **5**.
On **SUNDAYS**, *Morning*, half-past 7, *Afternoon*, at 5.

FARES:
To or from Aylesbury and London, - - - First Class, 11s.   Second Class, 7s. 6d.
8 JUNE 1839.

HOWSON, Printer, 38. Barbican.

Horse and mule drawn wagons of H. Devereux & Sons unloading coal from the wagons on No.2 coal road for Aylesbury Power
Station.

Geoff Williams

An Aylesbury panorama, immediately right of centre the steam shed and goods yard, in fact the original station site. In the centre the gasworks and sweeping round to the left the new station of 1889. From this station the council yard on the extreme left was served by a siding. This photograph of the 1920s was taken from the footbridge at Park Street Crossing (Dropshort). The short headshunt where the sheeted wagon is held is ludicrously ineffective. Note the rolls of wagon sheets on the ground alongside the siding where the oil tank wagons are.

L&GRP Courtesy of David & Charles

Enamel signs and the name 'Aylesbury High Street' places the date after September 1950. The translucent gas lamps of portmantau days have their delicacy palled in wartime black. Beloved of the LNWR these lamps graced many of their senior stations with the etched name facing the platform of arriving trains. The familiar Palethorpes', too, evokes the fifties era. On the left the van is parked in what was originally referred to as the horse dock.

L&GRP Courtesy of David & Charles

STOCK LAKE AYLESBURY

Bunker first working for the LNWR 2-4-2 tank with its rake of four six-wheel coaches seen from the Cheddington side of the Dropshort footbridge. Note the pair of inner home signals for the goods yard and the station one in the 'off' position.

Ken Hall

Local railway and bus guide of 1950 showing the service on the branch three years before the end of the passenger service, which remained virtually unchanged. The Leighton Buzzard to Dunstable service ended in April 1965.

Author's Collection

CHEDDINGTON - AYLESBURY													British Railways Table 5								
Third class only																					
WEEKDAYS ONLY																					
						SO	WSO														
Cheddington	7 32	9 15	11 10	1 25	2 20	4 25	5 43	7 35	8 35	....	....	....	....	..	...	...	....	...	....	....	..
MARSTON GATE	7 38	9 21	11 18	1 31	2 26	4 31	5 48	7 40	8 43	..	....	...	...	....	...	..	....	...	....	...	..
AYLESBURY *LMR*	7 47	9 30	11 33	1 40	2 35	4 40	5 57	7 49	8 56	..	...	..	..	....	..	..	....	..	...	..	..
					SO	WSO				SX											
AYLESBURY *LMR*	6 40	8 5	9 55	1 0	1 55	4 0	5 0	6 35	6 40	8 5	..	..	..	...	...	..	....	...	....	....	..
MARSTON GATE ..	6 49	8 14	10 4	1 10	2 4	4 9	5 9	6 43	6 48	8 14	..	..	..	....	....	..	....	...	....	....	..
Cheddington	6 55	8 20	10 10	1 16	2 10	4 15	5 15	6 49	6 54	8 20	..	..	..	....	....	..	....	...	....	....	..
SO–Saturday only. SX–Saturday excepted. WSO–Wednesday and Saturday only.																					

LEIGHTON BUZZARD - DUNSTABLE							British Railways Table 6						
Third class only													
WEEKDAYS ONLY							**WEEKDAYS ONLY**						
											SO	MF	
Leighton Buzzard	7 30	12 54	5 33	7 45	....	....	Dunstable *LMR* ...	8 46	1 16	6 5	6 10	8 21	....	..
Stanbridgeford	7 38	1 2	5 41	7 54	...	..	Stanbridgeford ...	8 52	1 22	6 13	6 18	8 27	....	..
Dunstable *LMR* ..	7 46	1 10	5 49	8 1	...	..	Leighton Buzzard ..	9 1	1 31	6 22	6 27	8 36	....	..
MF–Monday to Friday only. SO–Saturday only.													

BUILDERS AND ELECTRICAL ENGINEERS	**H. J. & A. WRIGHT LTD.**	GT. MISSENDEN TEL. No. **256**

79

However, it was a few years later in 1851 that all existing railways met their first great opportunity with the opening of the Great Exhibition in Hyde Park, London in May that year. Aylesbury station took its turn with Oxford, Banbury and Bedford for on the 21st July something like a thousand people assembled there to entrain in thirty carriages en route for the acclaimed palace of glass. August saw another six hundred taking the same route. The tiny station buildings and restricted platforms must have been hard pressed to handle such workings.

In such a vigorously contrasting age of industrial boom and poverty the railways could only introduce the prospective freedom of movement, and possible choice. Although it would be 50 years before the fare tariffs would be anything like acceptable to the daily work routine, with the exceptions of companies like the Great Eastern Railway with their cheap workmen's tickets. Those brave or desperate enough to book on third class trains where they existed would have had a raw experience up until 1844 and the introduction of

Gladstone's Regulation of Railways Act. Before then the London & Birmingham tacitly hauled third class passengers in open seatless wagons for 14s 0d (70p) for the entire length of the line which could hardly be regarded as a charitable dispensation. Mercifully the new act not only insisted on a covered train with seats calling at all stations but reduced the fare to 9s 6d (47$\frac{1}{2}$p) as a result of the 'penny a mile' clause. The only snag to that was when a passenger had booked upon one of these 'parliamentaries' as they were called. If he missed his connection at Cheddington he was effectively stranded or in a position of having to pay the excess.

Although Aylesbury can hardly be considered to be in the van of industrialisation, for it has never been assailed by the demands of heavy industry, it has nevertheless maintained a leading role through the seminal influence of the printing press which became Aylesbury's contribution to economic expansion in the 19th century.

In terms of trade the town was bound to have some strategic importance. It is first mentioned in Saxon times as being positioned along the Roman Akeman Street developing as a radial point for roads to Bedford, Oxford, Banbury and of course to London. A station on the first great main line of railway was just what it needed but in the event this was to be denied for a mere seven miles. Nevertheless the determination of its business community attempted to remedy this very quickly with the branch line connection. To begin with the L&B were lukewarm to goods trains which they sent along the branch attached to passenger workings which

With the outbreak of the First World War the Chilterns were affected early with gunnery ranges. By mid-September 1914 1,600 men had been billeted in the small market town of Tring, plus another 1,000 or so in nearby villages. This column heading out of the town past the LNWR station may have been amongst that number. These are part of Kitchener's new army, the 3rd Bucks. Territorials. Note how, when passing through the towns civilians are encouraged to join the column and the men are smoking and looking about them, which was quite a remove from normal marching discipline. Incredible to see cows in the High Street, and the man with them wears the armband of reserved occupation. Many agricultural workers were exempt from service in the early days of the war.

Bucks County Museum

Afternoon sunlight at Stocklake in the 1920s as a 2-4-2 tank with the usual assembly of LNWR six-wheelers is signalled by the inner home.

Geoff Williams

Waiting with loco coal at Dropshort siding is 2-4-2 tank No.46601 in 1950. Habitué of the Bletchley branches this engine in particular served the Aylesbury all its life and eventually hauled the last train.

C.R.L. Coles

On Manoeuvres, Squadron of Lancers entering Aylesbury.

Aylesbury High Street in 1912 as a squadron of Lancers enter the town past the LNWR station. The relaxed pedestrian appreciation along the street is remote beyond comparison with the motor vehicles almost endlessly using this main thoroughfare nowadays.

Bucks County Museum

would be a restriction on requirements. A charge for cattle at £1 a head from Aylesbury to Harrow would have been no great encouragement to graziers.

Before the arrival of Hazell & Watson's press the economy had been totally agrarian for centuries becoming industrial with the canal age to some degree then, with accelerating force with the introduction of the railway. The demand for fresh dairy produce in London was developing as rapidly as its population and here the railways had a special role to play. Many farmers in the area began to turn from sheep to dairy farming. This was further enforced with the repeal of the corn laws and the cheaper imported wheat causing arable farmers to turn to milk and butter also. In this force of change the Vale of Aylesbury had a central role to play.

The civic expansion of Aylesbury had been gradually taking place from early in the 19th century. A famous local railway promoter, Sir Harry Verney, together with his relative Florence Nightingale, greatly expanded the Royal Bucks Hospital in 1859. As Member of Parliament for Aylesbury Sir Harry served town and county well during his long life in addition to initiating the railways.

Perhaps less warmly applauded was the sombre expansion of the Aylesbury Union Workhouse that threw its shadow of desperate remedy over the elderly, infirm and foundling poor of the district.

In 1847 a Major Jebb of the Royal Engineers drew up and supervised the building of a more desperate institution of correction, Aylesbury Gaol, which was built adjoining the branch on Bierton Hill near the 6 milepost. It was eventually enlarged and became a prison for female malefactors.

Immediately preceding the building of the railway Aylesbury Gasworks brought its incandescent glow through its ancient streets. Oddly a siding was not built when the railway opened, presumably it was not considered necessary by gasworks or railway who would be required to share the expense, or did not see much justification when handling was cheap. A likely change of heart had occurred by 1899 when a siding was put in

A remarkable plan view of one of the earliest branch lines stations, dated 18th October 1841. Although for the proposed carriers sheds and cattle landing it shows how the station probably looked in the period of London & Birmingham operation. The section view of the goods shed, Fig. 1 is at first puzzling when related to Fig. 3 as it appears odd to build the platform so high above the solebar of the wagon. This is partly because a bad example is shown, using a covered wagon which probably only had end loading doors and would require an end loading dock. Most goods stock would be flat trucks or low open wagons, the latter being level with the top of the staging. Note the position of the engine house on the plan, this was moved shortly afterwards over to the carriage road to release space for coal drops.

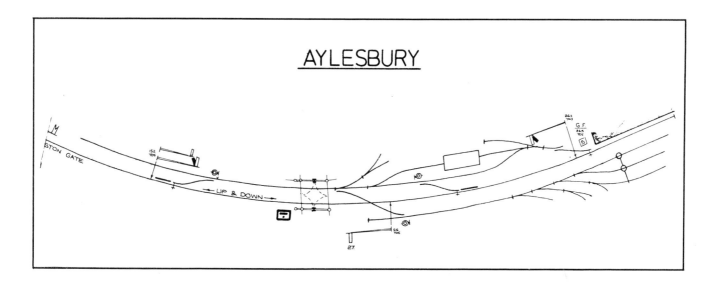

Although the soldiery and their meat dishes are the focal point of the photograph the location is of historical interest. It is station road, the thoroughfare leading to the entrance of the first railway terminus of 1839 which can be seen over the shoulders of the men at the end of the street. By 1914 it had become the entrance to the cattle and goods yard as it had been supplanted by the new station on the High Street.

Bucks County Museum

The celebrated 'Super D' class of 0-8-0 represented by No.49144 in Aylesbury goods yard in the summer of 1950. They resolutely carried the LNWR profile right up to the early 1960s at Bletchley shed where they were greatly cherished by the men that had to call on their efforts daily.

C.R.L. Coles

Aylesbury Coal Merchant F.J. Davis' smartly turned out new wagon. Complete with the commendable practice of the Gloucester Railway Carriage & Wagon Company of photographing the colour scheme alongside the wagon. In this case, dark green base with yellow panel and black name lettering; other lettering yellow with black shading.

Historical Model Railway Society/Gloucester Railway Carriage & Wagon Co.

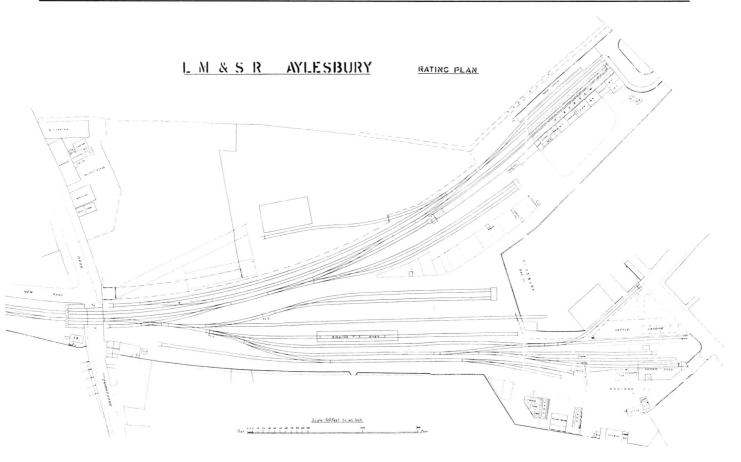

L M & S R AYLESBURY RATING PLAN

Scale 40 feet to an inch

Aylesbury station in its final form including the siding into the gasworks from the original station site, and the siding from the second station into the council yard that was added after the Second World War. Visible also is the former LNWR basket works and of course the problem of the arrangement of the notorious Dropshort (Park Street) level crossing.

G.K. Fox Collection

to the retort house from what had become the goods yard, as by that time a new station had been built for passenger services.

The demand for coal was certainly increasing but was hardly met. The L&B had at first been reluctant to disturb the flow of their lucrative passenger trains but the demand for coal was bound to carry weight. That being said the space allocated at Aylesbury was practically non-existent in terms of coal wharfage space and it is no surprise to see in 1848, that whilst Tring had 613 tons and Dunstable, opened during that year, had 8,263 and Leighton Buzzard had 971, the town of Aylesbury had a meagre 459. Clearly this had to be remedied, especially in view of the fact that railway cartage was halving that of canal from 2s 6d (12^1/2p) cwt to 1s 3d (6^1/2p).

In 1856 the locomotive shed was demolished and resited over the carriage storage road in order to free more land for the storage of coal. Nevertheless whilst the railway was a local concern its expansion was restricted and only really developed further with the purchase of it by the LNWR. Possibly the considerable length of the steam shed, 150 feet, was to enable it to

hold carriages also as it had utilised the carriage siding. In 1860 a new siding was put in for six wagons and in May 1861 600sq yards were made available for Messrs Locke & Moores at £20 per annum for coal storage. It is perhaps nowadays not so easy to appreciate the obsessive need for winter warmth suffered by our ancestors in this damp climate.

Communications developments were highlighted in a dramatic way in the year after the Great Exhibition when the local press reported an incident of great novelty in terms of criminal apprehension. A man committed a robbery at Aylesbury and used the train as a means of escape. The police were aware of this and constable Cornoby rode with speed to Tring station where he used the electric telegraph to contact the police at Euston. The unwitting felon stepped into the hands of his captors on alighting the train at Euston. He had given no thought to the existence of the telegraph for which he would have more than ample time for contemplation thenceforth. The incident serves as a useful pointer to the installation of this device at Aylesbury station seven years later on 23rd July 1859. The local press jubilantly announced that "Aylesbury

Built and opened shortly before the new station was opened the Type 4 LNWR signal box with the Webb/Thompson lever frame. Apart from the junction box at Cheddington this in effect was the only signal box on the line. In LNWR days the name of the box would have the cast letters screwed separately on the wooden fascia above the brickwork. Evidently the LMS have brought it into Midland practice with wooden letters on end panels.

Geoff Williams

The rather spartan interior of the Aylesbury box. The two levers pulled forward release the gatelocks, returning them against road or railway after moving them with the wheel.

Geoff Williams

This rather less familiar glimpse from the platform end is unique insomuch as it illustrates the period of the council yard siding and the appropriate signal, together with the semaphore for the platform starter. In the distance can be seen the original L&B cottages at Dropshort Crossing and some of the loco shed of the same company. The station frame released from the signal box can be seen in the foreground at the end of the platform. The method of running round at the station can be easily appreciated from this print. With the locomotive at the buffer end of the train the coaches would be propelled backwards clear of the lefthand turnout in the middle distance where they would be held, the locomotive would then take a position immediately in front of the van whilst the coach brakes were released and they ran down a 1 in 160 gradient into the platform. The engine would then take up position at the platform end facing Cheddington.

Geoff Williams

As the operation of the passenger services were handed over to Leighton men in 1950 so the 2-4-2 tanks were supplanted by brand new Ivatt 2-6-2 tanks operating push-pull. In this view of 20th July 1951 No.41275 prepares to return to Cheddington.

T.J. Edgington

The only bridge over the line at Dropshort (Park Street). The style is familiar on the LNWR and there was one very similar at Verney Junction. The bridge was put in shortly after a serious accident on the crossing when an old man was killed in 1883. Up until that time the crossing was manned by a 'Bobby' who also operated the protecting signals from a small hut with the levers in the open.

Geoff Williams

was now in communication with London – indeed with all the world!" In consequence it may be possible to assume that this facility was at that time installed at each guarded crossing along the line as an aid to train control.

For the first 22 years the people of Aylesbury had little choice for passenger use and cartage but to accept whatever the railway company considered was practicable. By that time other companies were closing the gaps that remained in the country which would bring them into further competition with each other. As previously mentioned the Great Western broad gauge arrived under the device of one of its acolytes, the Wycombe Railway, in 1863 to compete for London traffic. The LNWR's monopoly was now firmly at an end.

For some time the patrons of the LNWR branch had been dissatisfied with the situation of Aylesbury station whose trains were subservient to the crowded schedules of the main line that was still with only single 'up' and 'down' lines with a goods relief line as far as Watford. They expressed their dissatisfaction in voluble terms.

On 12th May 1866 a memorial petition was sent by Acton Tindal, original solicitor for the Aylesbury Railway and now clerk of the peace. It was also signed by some 82 other local luminaries. The petition was to persuade the company to build a joint station in the town to ease the problems of passengers travelling between the LNWR station and the recent terminus of the Wycombe Railway (GWR) from Princes Risborough. It also points out that the present LNWR station was totally inadequate. At this time the Wycombe Railway was laid exclusively in the GWR broad gauge.

After falling on deaf ears another memorial in December 1867 was sent underlining the inadequate accommodation afforded by the present passenger station at Aylesbury.

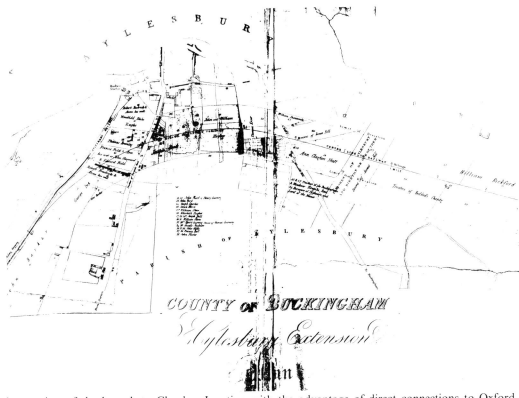

The proposed extension of the branch to Claydon Junction with the advantage of direct connections to Oxford, Banbury and Buckingham. Had this succeeded it would have affected Bletchley's development and the later Wycombe Railway that enabled Oxford to be reached via Princes Risborough.

John Pritchett Collection

One period during the day it was possible to see two engines on Aylesbury shed, No.7773 the Webb Coal tank with ex-Midland Class 4 0-6-0 freight engine which has just brought in the daily goods from Bletchley. Photographed late in the LMS period, just after the war.

Jack Turner

Early days of the 20th century at Stocklake. Empty roads and the high point of railway service with eleven trains each way on weekdays. Even the tank engines that hauled them were only a youthful 15 years old.

Osterfield Collection, Bucks County Record Office

The unmistakable feature of a LNWR weather boarded goods shed at Aylesbury with a grounded van body of the same company at the side. This view looking from the stables is dated August 1957.

Geoff Williams

"Therefore beg to summit to the Board that it would greatly be to the advantage of the undersigned and to the town of Aylesbury if arrangements were made for a joint station for the use of respective lines into the town." Signed Mr R.E. Eagles, Magistrate.

This appeal is born out of the frustrations of the Aylesbury and Buckingham's failed cause and should at least be partly directed to Harold Lepper, proprietor of the Bear Inn for had his property been bought and demolished there would have been nothing to stop the connection across Aylesbury going ahead and probably the development of one central station newly designed with adequate facilities. A change of gauge was imminent for the Wycombe Railway.

Evidence of the serious intentions of the LNWR are revealed in the plans drawn up which show the new connecting line starting to divide from the branch at Dropshort traversing over the land that was purchased from Sir Astley Cooper and Lord Carrington and would be used later for the new terminus station. It continued to cross the High Street and run parallel south of

The odd angle of the goods shed to provide road clearance into the goods yard is evident in this photograph. According to early photographs the lean-to office section with the single brick chimney could be of the London & Birmingham period.
Geoff Williams

Aylesbury station from 1839 to 1889. It is interesting to compare this with the plan of 1842, this survey being dated 1874. The problems of a restricted site are obvious. In order to meet the demand for coal the locomotive shed was moved from its northern position to the one shown here. This enabled the former shed road to become a coal siding adjacent to the stacking ground.
Ordnance Survey

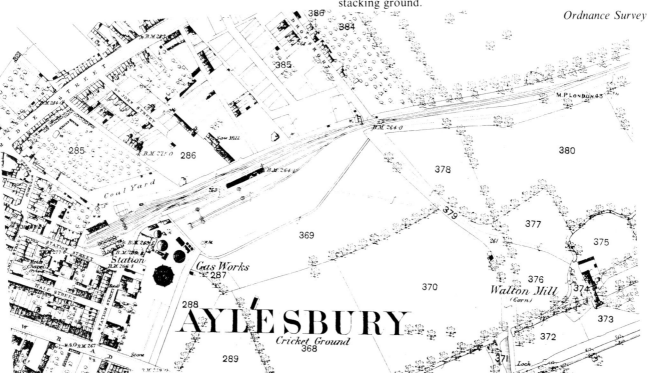

A view from the line near Stocklake towards the Aylesbury Prison.

Geoff Williams

Local timetable at the beginning of the 20th century showing
local connections, especially with regard to Cheddington.

T.J. Evans' Collection

42 L. & N.W.R. — To Bicester, Bletchley, Aylesbury, Harrow,
Watford, Tring, & London (Euston). WEEK DAYS.   SUN.

STATIONS.	a m	a m	a m	m p	m p	m p	n p	m p	m p	m p	m p	m p	m p	m p	m
OXFORD ...... dep	7 45		9 45	1050		12 0	1255	2 25		4 40	5 46	7 25		7 15	
Islip .... ,,	7 57		9 57			1212		2 37		4 51		7 37		7 26	
Bicester .... ,,	8 9		10 9	11 8		1223	1 13	2 50		5 2	5 57	7 49		7 37	
Launton .... ,,	8 14		1014		a			2 55		5 7		7 54		...	
Marsh Gibbon ,,	8 19		1019			1231	3 0			5 12		7 59		7 45	
Claydon........ ,,	8 28		1027			1239	3 8			5 19		8 7		7 53	
Verney Junction arr	8 35		1031			1243	3 11			5 22		8 11		...	
Verney Jun. dep	8 50		1050			1250	3 30			6 0		8 45		...	
Winslow Rd. ,,	8 55		1054			1254	3 35			6 4		8 48		...	
Grandboro'Rd ,,	9 0		1058			1259	3 40			6 9		8 52		...	
Quainton Rd ,,	9 9		1116			1 9	3 50			6 19		9 0		...	
Waddesdon M'n'r ,,	9 16		1121			1 14	3 55			6 23		9 4		...	
Aylesbury ...arr	9 25		1132			1 26	4 6			6 32		9 13		...	
Rickmansworth,,		1051	1228			2 20	5 5			7 24		1035		...	
Harrow .... ,,		11 8	1246			2 38	5 23			7 41		1053		...	
Wembley Park ,,		1130	1255			2 50	5 45			7 55		11 7		...	
Verney Junc. ...dep	8 37	8 40	1033			1244		3 12	3 21	5 25		8 12	8 21	...	
Winslow .... ,,		8 45	1040			1250		3 17	3 27	5 33		8 17	8 27	8 3	
Swanbourne ..... ,,		8 50	1045					3 31	...				8 31	8 c22	
BLETCHLEY ...arr	8 56	9 2	1055	1135		1 51	4 0	3 30	3 40	5 49	6 25	8 30	8 42	8 15	
BLETCHLEY ......dep	9 5	9 50	11 8	12 0	1219	2 30	1 57	4 9	4 20	6 50	6 30	9 5	9 55	8 45	
Leighton .... ,,	9 25	10 3	11 9		1222	2 42		4 20	4 33	7 2		9 17	10 7	8 57	
Leighton ...... ,,			1010			1225			4 45	7 10			1015		
Dunstable ..... arr			1027			1242			5 2	7 24			1039		
Luton (G.N.) ,,			1058			1 3			5 24	7 38			1055		
Hertford (G.N.),,			1242			2 16			6 48	9 57					
Cheddington ...arr	9 33	1013	1164		1230	2 51			4 42	7 10		9 26			
Cheddington dep		1040			1240	3 15			4 48	7 20		9 30			
Marston Gate arr		1047			1248	3 22			4 55	7 27		9 37			
AYLESBURY ,,		1055			1255	3 30			5 3	7 35		9 48			
Tring............dep		1023			1239	3 0			4 52	7 18		9 35		9 11	
Berkhamstead ... ,,		1032			1248	3 8			5 1	7 26		10 4		9 v23	
Boxmoor .... ,,		1041	12 e0		1257	3 15			5 7	7 35		1013		9v38	
King's Langley ,,		1050	12 e8		1 5	3 22			5 19			1021		9v47	
WATFORD JUN. arr		1056	12e14		1 11	3 28			5 25	7 45		9 52	1040	9 33	
WATFORD JN. dep		1133			1 35	3d40			5 30	7 50		10 0		...	
St. Albans .... ,,		1148			1 50	3d55			5 45	8 4		1018		...	
Willesden Junc. arr	10 9	1117	12e32	1249	1 33	3 47		2 43	5	15 47	8	5 7	17	9z37	1058	9 55
LOND'N (Euston),,	10b10	1130	12 01	5 1	50 4	5 2	55 5	15 6	5 8	20 7	30 9z50	1110	1010		

a Calls when required to pick up passengers.   b Dept. Bletchley 9.17 a.m.
c Leaves Winslow at 8.18 p.m.   * Calls to set down or pick up   † Leave Tring 9.55 p.m.

L. & N.W.R. — Bletchley, Buckingham, & Banbury WEEK DAYS.   SUN.

STATIONS.	a m	a m	p	m p	m p	m p	m p	m	a m	m
BLETCHLEY dep	8 20	1015		1 20 4	20 5	6 6	45	...	...	1135
Swanbourne ... ,,	B	1026		1 30	...	5 16	...	...	...	1146
Winslow ...... ,,	8 33	1033		1 36 4	35 5	21 6	59	...	...	1151
Verney Junc.... arr	8 37	1037		1 40 4	40 5	25 7	3	...	...	...
Verney Junc.... dep	8 39	1050		1 42 4	50 5	27 7	5	...	...	...
Padbury .... ,,	8 44	1057		1 47 4	57 5	34 7	10	...	...	1210
Buckingham ... arr	8 49	11 4		1 52 5	2 5	39 7	15	...	...	1217
Fulwell,&Westbury ,,	8 59	1116		2 2	...	5 53 7	28	...	...	1227
Brackley ...... arr	9 7	1123	1131	2 10	...	6 5 7	36	...	...	1234
Farthinghoe ,,	9 17		1146	2 21	...	6 22 7	47	...	...	1246
BANBURY ...... ,,	9 25	stop	1155	2 30	...	6 32 7	55	...	...	1255

a Calls to set down passengers from London on notice being given.
to Guard at Bletchley.
B Calls to pick up passengers for the Banbury line only.

EVRALL'S

Reliable Iron-frame Trichord
7-Octave
- PIANOS -
at **£15 15s.**
Cannot be beaten.

Cash or Weekly Payments taken.

14b, St. Ebbe's
and
19, St. Aldate's
—Oxford.—

L. & N.W.R. — From London (Euston), Tring, Watford, Harrow, **43**
Aylesbury, Bletchley, & Bicester. WEEK DAYS.   SUNDAYS.

STATIONS.	a m	a m	a m	a m	a m	p m	p m	p m	p m	p m	p m	m	a m
LONDON (Eustn) dp	6 10	7 10	7 20	8 35	1010	1220	1 45	2 45	5 0	5 35	7 10	8 d 0	9 0 10 0
Willesden Junc. ,,	6 23	...	7 41	8 47	1024	1232	1 57	2 57	4 29	5 48	7 22	...	9 13 1013
St. Albans....... ,,				8 40		1157	2 0		4 15		6 48		... 1010
WATFORD JN. arr				8 54		1211	2 14		4 29		7 2		... 1023
WATFORD JUN. dep	6 46		8 17	9 6		1255	2 21		5 26		7 42		9 36 c
King's Langley ,,	6 54		8 25			1238	2 29		5b17		7 50		9 44 ...
Boxmoor .... ,,	7 3		8 34			1 7	2`38		5b25		7 59		9 52 ...
Berkhamstead ... ,,	7 12		8 44			1 15	2 47		5b33		8 8		10 0 ...
Tring............ ,,	7 21		8 55			1 25	2 55		5 46		8 16		1010 ...
AYLESBURY ...,,	7 5			9 10		1 10	2 15		5 30		8 0		10 0 ...
Marston Gate ,,	7 15			9 19		1 19	2 26		5 39		8 9		10 9 ...
Cheddington ,,	7 22			9 25		1 26	2 33		5 45		8 15		1015 ...
Cheddington ....dep	7 30			9 31		1 34	3 6		5 55		8 24		1020
Hertford (G.N.) dp						9 25	1 20				5 45		...
Luton (G.N.) ,,	6 25		8 40	8 40		1220	2 40				7 55		...
Dunstable .... ,,	7 10		8 58	8 58		1 53	0				8 13		...
Leighton .... ,,	7 30		9 12	9 12		1 22	3 15				8 27		...
Leighton ....dep	7 40		9 17	9 40		1 44	3 20		6 3		8 35		1030 ...
BLETCHLEY ...... arr	7 50		9 26	9 49	1112	1 54	3 30	3 49	6 13	6 35	8 45	8 57	1040 1111
BLETCHLEY ...... dep	8 25			1015	1125	2 10	3 24	4 20		6 55		9 5	... 1135
Swanbourne ...... ,,	8 39			1026		2 21	c		7 8		e		1146
Winslow .... ,,	8 44			1033		2 26		4 35		7 14		9 17	1151
Verney Junc....arr	8 48			1037		2 31		4 40		7 18			...
Wembley Park dp	6 23		8 8			1210		2 30		4 55			...
Harrow .... ,,	6 30		8 14			1234		2 45		5 20			...
Rickmansworth,,	6 47		8 31			1251		3 2		5 22			...
Aylesbury ,,	7 45		9 20			1 41		3 50		6 23			...
Waddesdon M'n'r ,,	7 54		9 31			1 53		3 59		6 34			...
Quainton Road ,,	7 59		9 35			1 58		4 3		6 39			...
Grandboro' Rd.,,	8 7		9 46			2 10		4 11		6 47			...
Winslow Road ,,	8 11		9 51			2 14		4 15		6 51			...
Verney Junct. arr	8 15		9 55			2 18		4 18		6 55			...
Verney Junc. ...dep	8 50			1042		2 32		4 41		7 20			...
Claydon .... ,,	8 56			1047		2 38		4 47		7 25			12 0
Marsh Gibbon ,,	9 2			1054		2 45		4 55		7 32			12 7
Launton .... ,,	9 7			1058		2 50		5 0		7 37			1212
Bicester .... ,,	8 M 9 13			11 4	1152	2 54	9 5	6	7 45		9 37		1218
Islip .... ,,	8 M17 9 25			1115		3 8		5 18		7 57		e	1231
OXFORD .... ,,	8 M30 9 35			1125	1210	3 20	4 30		8 10		10 0		1245

M Rail Motor, one class only.   b Depart 16 minutes earlier on Saturdays.
c Calls when required to pick up passengers for Oxford Line on notice
being given at station. d dep. London 7.10 p.m. Sats. e Calls to set down on giving
notice to guard, and pick up on giving notice at station. d Sats. excepted

L. & N.W.R. — Banbury, Buckingham, and Bletchley WEEK DAYS.   SUN.

STATIONS.	a m	a m	noon	m p	m p	m p	m p	m p	m p
BANBURY ....dep	7 40	9 40		2 35		4 55	7 30	7 30	
Farthinghoe ,,	7 50	9 47		2 42		5 2	7 39	7 37	
Brackley .... ,,	8 6	10 0	12a0	2 55	4	5 21	7 52	7 50	
Fulwell & Westbury ,,	8 14	1016	612a6	3 1	4 11	5 30	7 58	7 56	
Buckingham .... ,,	8 27	1016	12a18	3 11	4 20	4 20 5	45 8	9 8	5
Padbury .... ,,	8 32	1020	12a21	3 15	4 25	4 25 5	48 8	13	e
Verney Junction ... arr	8 38	1025	12a27	3 20	4 29	4 29 5	54 8	18	
Verney Junction...dep	8 40	1027	1244	3 21	4 30	4 30 5	56 8	21	
Winslow ...... ,,	8 45	1033	1250	3 27	4 34	4 34 6	1 8	27	8 18
Swanbourne ... ,,	8 50		1 2			6 6	8 31	8 22	
BLETCHLEY ...... arr	9 2	1045	1 5	3 40		6 20	8 42	8 33	

a Thursdays excepted. c Calls to set down, and pick up passengers
for beyond Bletchley. e Calls if required to pick up passengers

EVRALL'S for

Singer's, Wheeler &
Wilson's, Jones Co.'s
and Kholer's

Hand & Covers
from **£2/15/-**

Cash or Weekly Payments taken.

14b, St. Ebbe's,
—Oxford.—

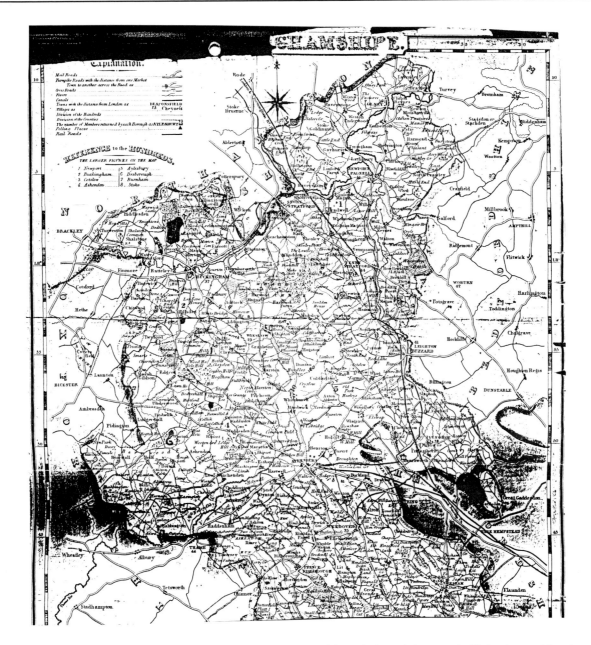

Map of 1836 showing the competing line to Aylesbury from Tring, ultimately intended to reach Cheltenham with a branch to Oxford north of the city. Had Stephenson not revised the scheme to bring the line no closer than the village of Bishopstone it is possible that all the advocates would have united their interests and the line to Aylesbury would have been as seen here. Whether this would have benefited the aspirations of the Cheltenham lobby to the extent of succeeding in reaching the spa town is an open question.

Aylesbury County Library

Exchange Street; passed over the Wendover Road (site of the Bear Inn) then swept round facing north in a 1 furlong 5 chain radius curve to bring it parallel with the site of the existing station. Upon the failure of this one property purchase the LNWR withdrew.

Impending developments on the main line would ensure that Aylesbury would have ten passenger trains 'up' and 11 'down' by 1894. It also remained the main access route to the North. It is with the opening of the Metropolitan line to Aylesbury in 1892 and the Great

Central Railway extension in 1898 that the balance swings markedly in the direction of the new station.

The new LNWR station opened on Sunday 16th June 1889 whilst the old station officially closed to passenger usage the day before. When it had been been opened Aylesbury's population stood close to 5,000, it having been variously checked by emigration and agricultural depression but had steadily risen to 9,000 when the new station opened.

Pair of semi-detached cottages at Dropshort for the signalmen that worked a two shift arrangement. Actual date of construction cannot be stated with certainty but as they were required when the line opened it must be assumed that these are of the 1839 period.

Geoff Williams

Aylesbury High Street on 19th July 1952. As a passenger station the building had but seven months to serve when this photograph was taken.

H.C. Casserley

A royal visit took place on Thursday 12th July 1883 when King Edward VII was Prince of Wales. He arrived by special train at the old Aylesbury station of the LNWR on his way to Waddesdon Manor which was still under construction. The towns people set up a special fund to buy a profusion of bunting streamers and placards to assure the Prince that his arrival at Aylesbury would be loyally recognised. Even the gasworks contributed to the ambiance of the situation by supplying 10,000cu feet of gas free to illuminate the decorations by night. Morosely the LNWR gave no special instructions nor were there any budgeting allocations to decorate the station, although in the normal company representations the arrival of a royal train was greeted courteously and the old station was presented in a neat and polished condition.

The plans for the new station at Aylesbury are dated 6th June 1888, and they compare interestingly with the design of the original one, although it must be admitted that the original station underwent several modifications in its time. It was built in brick with the single platform under a glazed canopy enclosing one set of rails and supported on the track side by eight columns. With a comparatively short platform of 400ft on a restricted site, it was obviously decided to save space by not having the runround loop in the platform but, in the station approach area. The platform buildings occupied 200ft and were divided in an elementary way into the booking hall, booking office, parcels office, general waiting room, ladies' third class waiting room, ladies' second class waiting room and gents' first class waiting room. First class ladies would be required to cross the class lines whilst second and third class gents sufficed with the general waiting room. Adjoining these were the porters' room, stores, urinals, w.cs and a boiler house. The entrance door was placed in a 54ft wide brick facade.

No doubt the station when new presented a plain but businesslike approach to the service with administration of Stationmaster, five clerks, four porters, three carters and two signalmen. Trains would for many years comprise of four-wheel stock, some ex-L&B until the introduction of six-wheel stock in the 1900s. With a tank engine and four of these coaches a train would then be approximately 200ft long which would have been conspicuously cramped in the old L&B station.

Apart from the competitive edge of the rival railway facilities in the town and the considerable pressure put

Railway timetable published in the local newspaper in October 1868, a month after the opening of the Aylesbury & Buckingham line. Three trains each way daily just about constituted a service. The 12.35pm at Verney Junction had much time in hand before forming the 2.05pm departure. Note competing trains with LNWR to Oxford and Aylesbury on the GWR, yet the LNWR still supplied the most intensive service.
Bucks County Library

After the Great War many military vehicles were demobbed into civilian use, in effect accelerating the further utilisation of motor vehicles. Standing in the yard at Aylesbury is a Maxwell lorry, with its solid tyres and acetylene lighting. The colour scheme is blue with red wheels and white lettering.

Courtesy Devereux & Sons

Four warehousemen from Dominion Dairy that was close by Aylesbury station, and shipped much of their famous Golden Acre butter over its metals. Behind them the fine livery of an LNWR 45ft van is clearly seen. Left to right: George Sibley, Arthur Clarke, Aron Brown and booking clerk Elmer.

Billy Sutton courtesy Geoff Williams

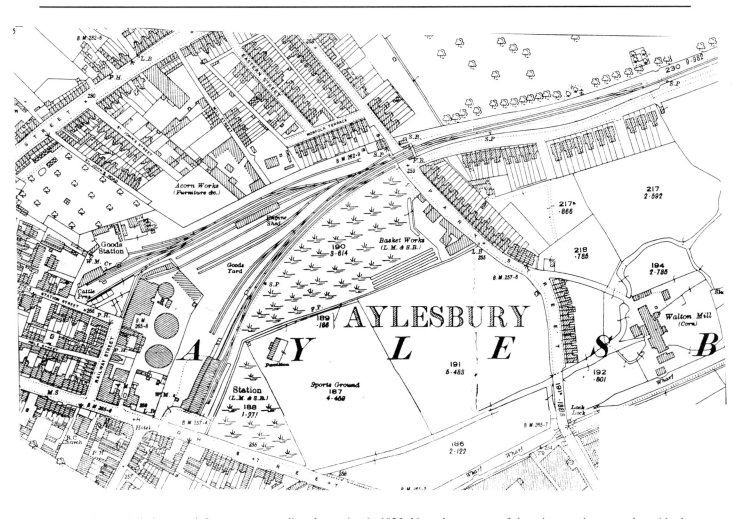

The situation at Aylesbury and the area surrounding the station in 1925. Note the expanse of the osier growing area alongside the station that eventually became the council yard and had its own siding.

Ordnance Survey

on the LNWR to improve their passenger facilities, the need for better accommodation for four-footed beings had become lamentable. The old cattle landing of 50ft in length, between the sidings of the old station, was to be supplanted by the use of the original passenger platform which would provide length and pen facilities for no less than twelve cattle wagons. A new platform facing the passenger platform in the new station was designated as a horse landing and end-loading dock.

A certain ingenuity in working trains was applied by the operating staff which may not have had the sanction of the working appendix but nevertheless continued without stricture. A glance at the maps will show that the passenger run-round loop was inconveniently placed. In order to minimise the use of this the train staff utilised the falling grade just beyond the gates of 1 in 160 which levelled in the platform space. A train arriving at the platform first discharged its passengers and then reversed along its path until clearing the first left-hand point. The engine would then uncouple and reverse into the siding through the points which were then reset for the platform road. The guard would then release his handbrake and the coaches would roll into the platform for the engine to return to the end facing departure. All of this would be accomplished using the ground frame at the platform end that was released by bolt from the signal box lever No. 21. All of this would save time rather than use the loop.

It is a tragic irony that the course of human endeavour is often precluded by accident and disaster. Railway development takes its place with other industries in this, the torturous paths to full train braking and block signalling bearing witness.

The irony is highlighted on such minor tributaries as the Aylesbury branch. A gruesome accident revealed not only the condition of the line from the point of view of safety but the methods employed in 1880, 40 years after the line had opened. Coincidentally the accident took place only seven days after the introduction of absolute block on the branch on the 18th November.

LONDON AND NORTH-WESTERN RAILWAY.
AYLESBURY BRANCH.

LEAVE.		WEEK DAYS.													SUNDAYS.		
	A.M.	A.M.	A.M.	A.M.	P.M.		P.M.	P.M.	P.M.		P.M.	P.M.		A.M.	A.M.	P.M.
AYLESBURY	7 58	12 9	9 15	1120	1 0	...	2 25	4 15	5 12	...	6 25	7 25	...	7 25	10 0	5 18
Marston Gate	7 15	8 23	*	*	*	...	*	*	5 22	...	6 35	7 35	...	7 35	10 9	5 28
Cheddington, arr. from Aylesbury	7 22	8 30	9 30	1137	1 18	...	2 43	4 30	5 29	...	6 42	7 42	...	7 42	1015	5 35
Leighton arrive	7 47	...	9 41	1220	1 34	...	3 22	4 41	5 44	...	7 0	8 38	...	...	1028	5 47
Willesden ,,	8 29	9 23	1012	1228	...	†	3 54	5 48	...	...	7 37	8 57	...	9 10	1 24	7 31
EUSTON ,,	8 42	9 35	1025	1240	...	†	4 10	6 0	...	...	7 50	9 15	...	9 32	1 45	7 50

LEAVE.		WEEK DAYS.													SUNDAYS.		
	A.M.	A.M.	A.M.	A.M.	P.M.	P.M.	P.M.	P.M.		P.M.	P.M.	P.M.	P.M.		A.M.	P.M.
EUSTON dept. for Aylesbury	6 0	7†30	9 15	1040	1215	...	1 45	3 15	...	4 15	5 45	6 0	7 10	...	9 0	2 30
Willesden ,,	6 18	7 42	9 26	1058	1226	...	1 57	3 26	...	4 27	5 56	6 11	7 20	...	9 12	2 49
Leighton ,,	7 13	8 27	9 56	1135	12 5	...	2 43	4 30	...	...	6 40	7 40	...	...	7 38	4 15
Cheddington ,,	7 45	8 45	1040	1215	1 30	...	3 15	4 45	...	5 38	6 51	7 8	8 35	...	1025	4 28
Marston Gate ,,	7 52	8 52	1047	*		...	3 22	*	...	5 45	¶	*	...	...	1032	4 35
AYLESBURY arrive	8 2	9 2	1057	1232	1 44	...	3 32	5 2	...	5 55	7 20	8 53	...	...	1042	4 45

PASSENGERS FROM AYLESBURY should note the time the Aylesbury Trains reach Cheddington, and then refer to the Main Line Tables to ascertain the time the Main Line Trains leave Cheddington, to continue their journey.

† Passengers by this train for Stations between Watford and Cheddington must change at Watford.

¶ The 7.5 p.m. train, Cheddington to Aylesbury, calls at Marston Gate when required to set down Passengers from London; also on Saturdays to pick up or set down.

Timetable for October 1894. Of particular interest are the trains operating from and into Leighton station which would enable cross-country connections via the Dunstable branch.

Robin Pallet

On 25th November one William Palmer proceeded to cross the line through a wicket gate at Dropshort level crossing. He was an old man that stooped, was known to be deaf as well as blind in one eye. As he crossed over the line he was struck and by the time the train had been brought to a halt it was found that the unfortunate man had all but been decapitated. What transpired at the inquest in the following December was the situation and the attitudes that dictated its inevitable occurrence.

The driver, one George Stevens of Mill Street, Aylesbury gave evidence that he saw him crossing the line when the engine was about ten yards away from him. He had immediately sounded the whistle but the man was impervious to the sound, and he managed to stop the train after it had dragged the body a further seven or eight yards. A short stopping distance was possible as steam had been shut off one mile before the terminus. The train was travelling at about 6mph and even though the patent brake was employed it still could not have been brought to halt any sooner.

The Coroner enquired if it would not have been a regulation to blow his whistle when approaching a crossing. Stevens replied that it was not customary to do so and he could not see any reason if you can see that the line is clear. To this the Coroner added further, "Anyone would not be so likely to cross if he did hear its sound from a hundred yards, very likely it would draw his attention". Obviously feeling gradually hemmed in by the Coroner's questions he referred to the company inspector who said that the drivers were not to blow their whistles unless they saw cause to do so as it was regarded as an abominable nuisance in the neighbourhood.

It seems incredible that so simple an expedient could be regarded so lightly, disregarding any pedestrian safety, especially for dark winter mornings and evenings with the frail illumination of oil lamps. In fact much was placed on the vigilance of the attendant crossing keeper/signalman and in the sub-division of this man's duties lay the inherent danger.

Charles James was the signalman stationed at Dropshort Gate. He stated that his position at that time was putting a distant signal in the 'on' position; he was standing about ten yards from the gate in the Cheddington direction. The object of the distant signal was to instruct the driver to shut off steam. There is a signal box close to the gate and the 'home' signal was situated on the opposite side of the line, whilst the lever by which it was worked was attached to its post. This necessitated him having to cross the line to work the signal. The distant signal was 1,000 yards from the box whilst the lever for working this was about ten yards from the box. On a train leaving Cheddington the signalman received a signal by telegraph, and he received another when it left Marston Gate. If the line was clear of traffic the man took 'off' the 'home' and 'distant' signals, the normal position for them being at 'danger'. He would return them to that position when the train passed. Clearly James could not work the signals and remain close to the crossing at the same time, albeit ten yards away. He would probably remain in situ until the train had passed him then cross over the line to place the 'home' on danger. This would give him no chance to physically apprehend anyone about to use the crossing.

An inspector giving evidence claimed that ten days previously the 'home' signal had been moved four or five yards closer to the gate and a lever for this signal put on the same side alongside the distant lever. This obviated the signalman having to cross the line to work the lever. Having done this after the accident and before the inquest it appears that the company were well aware of the incongruity of the arrangements at Dropshort and how they must look at the inquest. The inspector admitted that in putting the signal 'on' the man would have his back to the crossing. He did not know how long

The station front at about the time that the passenger service ceased.

V.R. Anderson

the side gates had been in existence at the crossing but he thought it to be about three or four years, they having been installed for the convenience of foot passengers. He could not positively say but thought that it had been done under public request to prevent persons having to wait. This makes it appear like a company concession to allow freedom of movement along the highway rather than fulfilling the requirements of the Act. He admitted that level crossings were gradually being done away with and bridges were being erected in lieu of them, as a matter of form. Locking the wicket gates would of course necessitate some alteration to them. It seems incredible that gates should not be locked and the fact that they were not is an admission of negligence. In the present time crossings without the watchful eye of a keeper, even with visual and audible alarms, have exacted a terrible toll.

A pretty bald statement by the company was that people using the gates were capable of looking after their own limbs. Further, that a company man was at the gate to manage the signals and caution the public. They believed that if the wicket gates were closed by mechanical means some people would climb over them, then if they were harmed, the cry would have been "why doesn't the company build a bridge!" Another witness claimed that the wicket gates had been installed for the convenience of the printing works and milk works, but the inspector stated that they were made before the printing works was started.

Signalman James was recalled to the witness box and had to admit that although the signal post had been moved and the lever put on the same side as the other lever when he operated them, his back was still towards the crossing. He admitted also that there was a good

deal of traffic over the crossing, and he often had to send children away from playing there.

The signalman had been in the employ of the company about three months and before coming here he had been at Willesden where he learned signalling. He saw the body after the accident, and said that the head was nearly severed from the trunk. The train was timed to leave Cheddington at 11.40am and reach Aylesbury at 11.55am. The average speed would be 30mph. Steam was usually shut off at Broughton Gates and after that it would take about $2^1/2$ minutes to get into the station. Coroner Mr Hinds adroitly pointed out that it would require a greater speed than 6mph. The Coroner's observation was correct as Broughton Crossing was virtually a mile from Dropshot and, allowing for the decrease in speed of shutting off steam and a few yards of brake application, the train would still be moving at something close to 25mph between the two locations.

In summing up he did not apportion blame to either driver, stoker or crossing keeper. Whether to make any suggestion about the crossing was a matter for consideration of the jury, the death was clearly the result of an accident.

The jury after some consideration returned a verdict of accidental death and in view of the increasing use of the crossing the company should afford some additional accommodation and means to caution the public for their safety. The Coroner promised to write to the company urging this recommendation with special reference to children. Out of expediency or pressure from the Board of Trade a footbridge was erected some three years later at this crossing.

The largest single employer in the town was the capacious business of the famous printing firm of

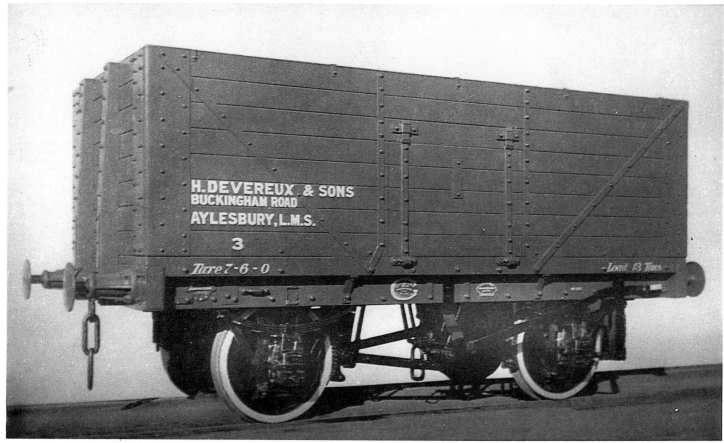

Devereux's wagon No.11 built by Gloucester Railway Carriage & Wagon Co. under a government subsidy after the Second World War. Details of sole bar registration plate: 1946 – No.17706 – LMS. Date of photograph: September 1946.

Geoff Williams

Hazell, Watson & Viney. Coincidentally their business was founded in London in precisely the same year that the Aylesbury Railway had opened. Starting with a tiny works of three employees in that year they eventually grew until they had capital assets of £1,000,000 and employed 1,700 a century later in 1939.

Discussions on moving to Aylesbury took place in 1866 with a plan to move to better working conditions and lower costs in the countryside. Aylesbury was probably attractive from the rail connection point of view as it now had access to the GWR and the West via High Wycombe, as well as the LNWR.

The firm's production list at this date is impressive, with works for John Ruskin, George Allen, Bacon's, Blackwoods, Chatto & Windus, Hodder & Stoughton, Lane's, Longmans, Macmillan, Morgan & Scott, John Murray, Routledge, Sunday School Union and William & Norgate. With such rapid expansion the original works close to the Met./GWR station was soon outgrown and a new works was opened and put into production in 1878 on the Tring Road. Within this new works was a room capable of seating 250 persons that served as a worker's institute and library. Obviously the firm took the progressive view that employee welfare

develops an enlightened workforce and a better member of the community rather than the wasteful recourse to habitual drink.

Over the succeeding years the plant gradually expanded introducing many new printing and binding techniques. Amongst the experiments was the introduction of a phonograph for corresponding verbally with London, for in 1894 there was no telephone service available in Aylesbury. Less successful was the attempt to supplant the use of the railways by introducing a steam lorry for the Aylesbury to London run in 1901. At an average speed of $2\frac{3}{4}$mph this was obviously doomed to fail. Nevertheless the die was cast, with road transport becoming a dramatically effective competitor 20 years later.

For loading in rail vans, books and magazines were packed in enormous permanent containers which they called 'kennels' and measured 10ft x 6ft x 4ft. By the mid-twenties the company's haulage began gradually to be partitioned in favour of some road transport. An interesting aside to the company's goods work was the import of strawboard for bookbinding from Holland. As late as 1939 this was brought up the branch of the Grand Union Canal to Aylesbury in narrow boats.

It is interesting to recount that beside the world famous *Reader's Digest* many other famous titles have rolled off the presses of Hazell, Watson & Viney. Fifty years ago came the first Penguin paperback titles followed by magazines like *Good Housekeeping, Harper's Bazaar, The Connoisseur, Homes & Gardens, Strand, Pearsons, Lilliput, Men Only* etc.

Another large employer in Aylesbury that was to become involved significantly with the local railways was the English Condensed Milk Company. Their factory employing 24 persons opened on the High Street on the 22nd August 1870. The novel Swiss process of condensing milk became very popular, especially for children and by 1880 the rich agricultural land of the district was supplying milk from 2,000 cows.

By now there were one hundred workers at the factory producing from the staple product sweetened condensed milk, sweetened coffee and milk, sweetened cocoa and milk, and also a coffee essence. Milk was brought by train from long distances, whilst consignments of condensed milk went from the station. By process of amalgamation it became known as the Anglo Swiss Condensed Milk Company. Eventually becoming the well known Nestlé Company in 1905 whose chocolate was a familiar adjunct to railway station refreshment facilities.

Heavy demand during the First World War for the armed forces saw tin plate arriving by canal boat which also carried out enormous tonnages of the manufactured goods.

The production of the condensed milk ceased in 1924 as there was a London-initiated demand increasing for fresh liquid milk. The factory continued to collect this in bulk and despatch it to London by rail. Pasturised milk was also produced from local dairymen and bottled for local retailers. From 1928 to 1941 cheese was produced whilst the milk processing continued up until 1961 when it was sold out and replaced with the new expanding

The wooden sign on the brick façade has weathered the period of the LNWR and LMS by the time that this photograph was taken of the station front at Aylesbury in September 1950 under British Railways ownership. It was not to survive much longer after this date, for although the station closed to passenger traffic in 1953 it was fitted with shiny new enamel maroon signs carrying the name 'Aylesbury High Street' in 1951. Parcel Porter of many years is Arthur Clarke, the man leaning on the bicycle.

V.R. Anderson

markets in dehydrated foods, in particular Maggi soups. The present factory produces a wide range of foods, including the trade name of Crosse & Blackwell, which are packed in tins, cartons, sachets and boxes. In the familiar trend the business is handled almost entirely by road transport. The cessation of milk marketing two years before the end of goods traffic on the Aylesbury branch underlines the conclusion of an amalgam of interests between the manufacturer and the means of distribution.

Emphasising still further the role of Aylesbury with dairy farming it is important to point out that although Nestlés may have been the major processor of these foods in the area they were by no means alone. Dominion Dairy on Park Street required considerable gallonage of milk to produce their cheese and butter output which almost exclusively used the branch, especially in the early days.

Another business that used the railway extensively was the Aylesbury Brewery (ABC) that had wagons of barley and hops brought down the line from 1895 until 1935; from then it became a bottling plant only. One signalman recalls a train of flat wagons each carrying two large covered vats, snaking its way quietly onto the branch, the train looked almost sinister until it was realised that within its dark enclosures lay the foamy gleam of Guinness on its way to be bottled in the Aylesbury brewery!

The straw plait industries of Bedford are not far away and an associated craft was started by the railway itself at Aylesbury, this being a basket weaving factory on Park Street. From here innumerable mail, hamper and carrying baskets were produced for the LNWR.

The factory was laid out in 1880, it including a single storey workshop building with ten windows facing the road. On each side of it were two arch-roofed buildings. A square shaped chimney stack protruded from the centre from the wash house and boiler for the heating chamber. The furthest arch roof building from the level crossing contained the beds of reed laid out for drying, whilst the shed nearest the crossing was for storing finished work. Osier beds adjoined the area and to some

degree actually grew along the trackside and men were employed to go up and down the line cutting them. The factory was designed to employ 20 persons and as there was only one toilet containing two urinals and two w.c.s presumably all employees were men.

The osier beds fell into disuse in the late 1930s but the factory continued with imported osiers until 31st December 1947 when it was finally closed down. The building was then used by W.F. Carlisle to store green bananas. The yard area came into council use in LMS days.

A great deal of cattle was brought down from the grazing farms that abound in the countryside around Aylesbury. This would bring long trains of cattle vans down the line to be shunted into position alongside the pens in the old station. By and large Aylesbury LNWR/LMS was no sleepy branch line terminus and much work was required with goods wagons keeping the morning goods shunting well into the afternoon before it could form its return working. In the early days this would continue unperturbed, but as Park Street became more urbanised, especially in the 20th century, there was mounting protest about the crossing. A signalman, Mr Ned Goodyer on duty at the crossing found his job more and more uncomfortable as irate motorists became impatient with the goods engines shunting over the road, piling abuse on the signalman. Certain footplatemen known to be of a taciturn disposition would glance impishly into car windscreens as they rolled back and forth.

In 1950 the routine of shunting coaches was discontinued with the introduction of push-pull working which did not require a guard but needed a driver and passed-fireman. Bletchley had three LMS push-pull sets, one for the Aylesbury line and one each for the Dunstable and Newport Pagnell lines. When any of these were taken out of service there was an antiquarian ex-LNWR set used.

On 25th September of the same year the station was suffixed 'High Street' whilst the other station became Aylesbury 'Town'.

Chapter 4

Marston Gate

Broughton Crossing where the road from Bierton to Broughton crossed the line. The crossing keeper's house is on the right, and this is almost certainly contemporary with the opening of the line in the L&B period. The chamfered walls on each side, for looking both up and down the line are reminiscent of the toll houses of the turnpike trust days. Date of photograph is 8th July 1959.

Geoff Williams

The only station between Cheddington and Aylesbury first appears in the company minutes for 27th March 1857, with reference to it as a possible railhead. This was affirmed some six months later when it was sanctioned to open as a goods station. Its development into a country station in the accepted sense appears to have been a gradual affair.

On 2nd May 1860 P.C. Bauce the gateman at Marston Crossing was reprimanded for allowing his gates to be run through on the morning of Sunday 8th April. Mr Bruyeres, Superintendent of the line requested of Mr McConnell, Locomotive Superintendent, to warn his drivers to stop at this gate as the man in charge had very long hours to keep, waiting for the return of the Saturday cattle trains whose time of returning was very uncertain.

On 4th July, Mr Woodhouse, contractor for works, was asked to assess the cost of a proper booking office at Marston Gate. This sounds as if tickets were being issued for passengers by the 'Bobby' and as goods tended to be attached to passenger trains, it is quite possible the company would have accepted this extra revenue at no inconvenience. On the 15th of the following August Mr Woodhouse reported back that he had assessed the cost of making a complete station at £210. He was referred back for his plan to be revised so as to give merely a booking office with a moderate amount of shelter from the weather. The amount of annual traffic was reported at the same time.

In September he submitted his revised estimate: Cost of Booking Office £73, Waiting Shed £48. Traffic to and from the station to Aylesbury and Cheddington, which

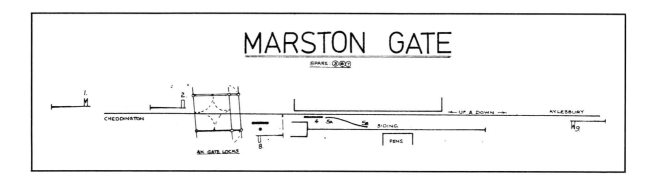

Broughton Crossing from the road side. The small hut on the right contained the crossing keeper's instruments and a telephone, there being no signals at Broughton. The prominent public house seems curiously outsize for this rural area, and it is believed to be associated with the Rothschilds.

Geoff Williams

A view from the guard's brake van between Marston Gate and Aylesbury. The concrete sleepers are interesting as they were laid by Dow Mac in 1942 when the company was testing their use. This photograph taken on 11th April 1962, after closure of the passenger service.

Geoff Williams

Ground plan of Marston Gate station c1930. The odd arrangement of placing the station buildings over a ditch was to allow for double track and siding expansion on the 'down' side. That was in the early 1860s, and in the event neither of these prospects came to fruition.

G.K. Fox Collection

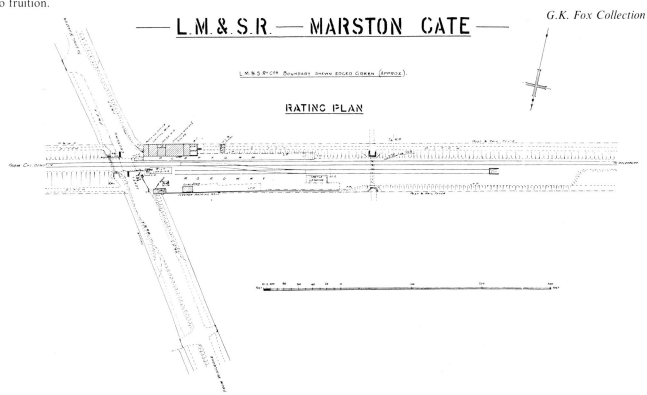

After the cessation of the passenger train services the station sign was removed, revealing some interesting early lettering.
Lens of Sutton

Marston Gate Crossing and station looking in the Aylesbury direction, from which the signal suggests a train is arriving. On the right is a small weighbridge office and lamp hut. The ticket office with block instruments was in the timber building adjoining the house. The sign on the end of the timber building is of the LNWR period whilst the signals are tubular steel British Railways upper quadrant. The date is 24th January 1953.

H.C. Casserley

Probably the last man to hold the post of Stationmaster at Marston Gate – Joseph Millar on the platform at Marston Gate. Note the timber platform on the 'up' side behind him that was used to stack milk churns.

Mrs MacGrath

were the only places booked to, was about £300 per year. The manager stated that any improvements made must be done so as not to interfere with the prospect of the line being doubled. It was resolved that the plans would be further considered in December. A strip of adjoining land that belonged to a Mr Williams would be required.

Nothing transpired then until the following June when it was minuted that the cottage for the 'Bobby' required repair. Also that some land adjoining held by a Mr Locksby was to be exchanged for a piece of land belonging to the company. The following September the company discovered that the land that they had hoped to exchange for that needed to build a station had been sold by them some six years earlier.

On 3rd July 1863 Mr Woodhouse was again prevailed upon to supply a revised estimate to supply "proper accommodation for traffic". Dutifully he supplied an estimate of £121.

What appears to be the final conclusion of all this indecision came on the 15th September 1864 when the plans were at last approved to build at Marston Gate Crossing a Booking Office and Stationmaster's house at a cost of £283, marked 'urgent'.

As Marston Gate station had appeared first in Bradshaws in 1860 and in the timetables of the local press in 1863 it becomes a matter of definition as to when it actually was opened as a station.

Finally, on 20th July 1865 the General Manager recommended that the land be purchased to erect a station signal and two distant signals at Marston Gate. The single pole at the crossing may well have held two semaphores for protection 'up' and 'down' the line, which was common practice in 19th century branch line and secondary line signalling. Bearing in mind the reference to leave space for possible doubling of the track, the timber platform at Marston Gate was built on timber piles above a ditch on the 'down' side, abutting this was the two-storied station building with living accommodation at platform level. A single siding was situated trailing from the 'up' side which was probably in situ before the station buildings when it was just a goods station, and there was also a milk landing platform at the end of this. A cattle dock was also situated on this side together with a loading gauge, and a small weighbridge, lamp hut and gas lamp. All of this was controlled from an eight-lever frame with Annette's key gatelocks which had to be locked into position with the gates across the road, before the frame could be released.

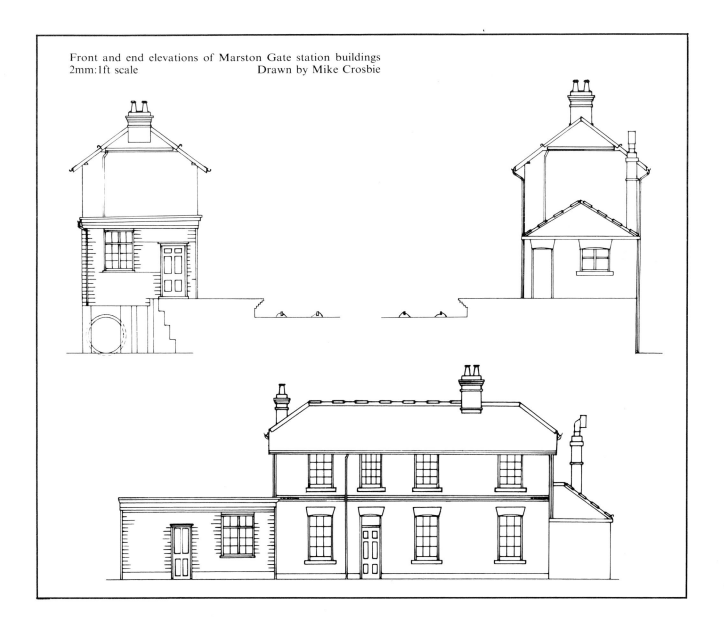

Front and end elevations of Marston Gate station buildings
2mm:1ft scale   Drawn by Mike Crosbie

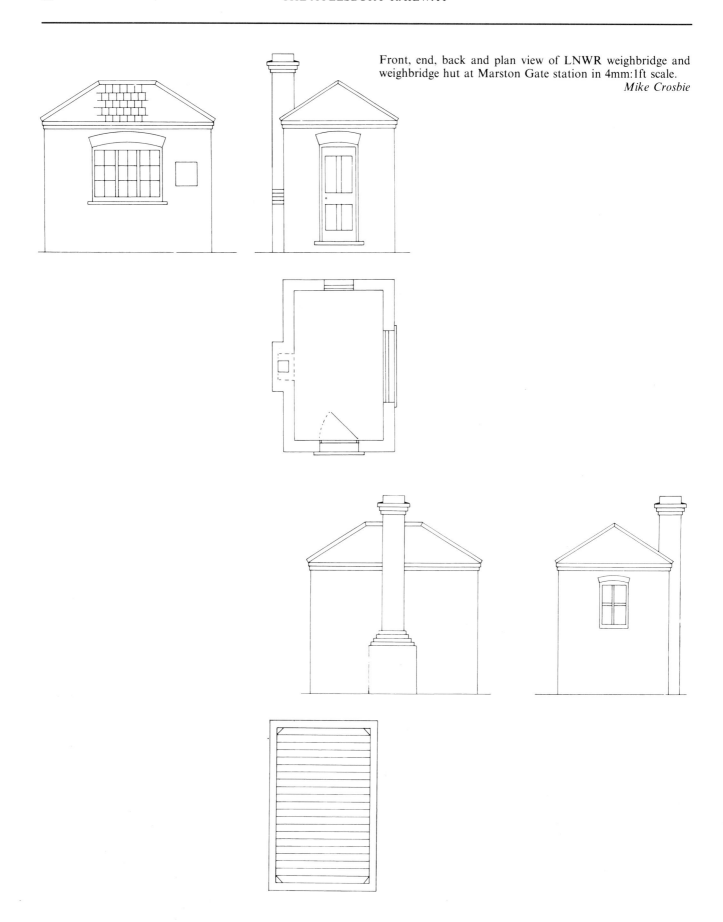

Front, end, back and plan view of LNWR weighbridge and weighbridge hut at Marston Gate station in 4mm:1ft scale.
Mike Crosbie

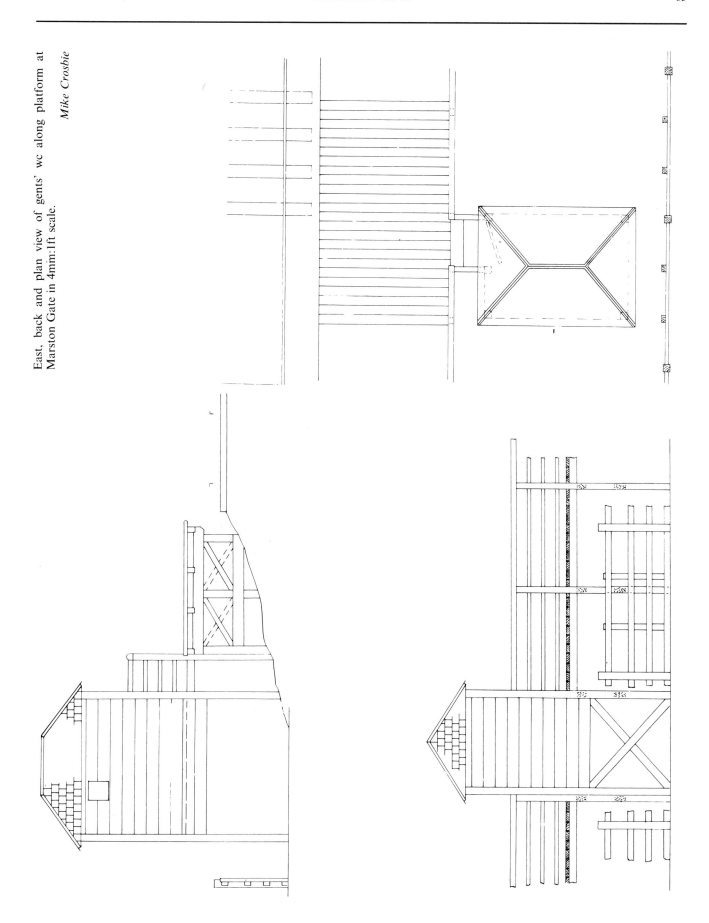

East, back and plan view of gents' wc along platform at Marston Gate in 4mm:1ft scale.

Mike Crosbie

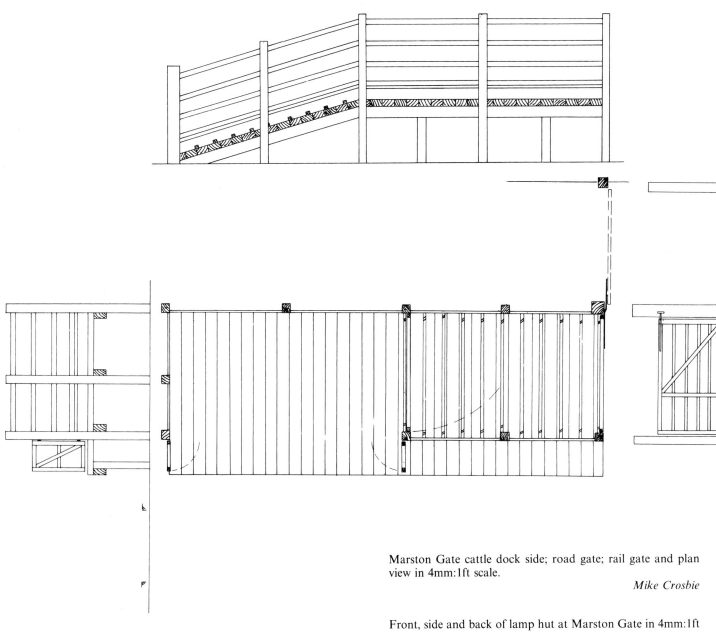

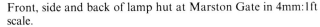

Marston Gate cattle dock side; road gate; rail gate and plan view in 4mm:1ft scale.

Mike Crosbie

Front, side and back of lamp hut at Marston Gate in 4mm:1ft scale.

Mike Crosbie

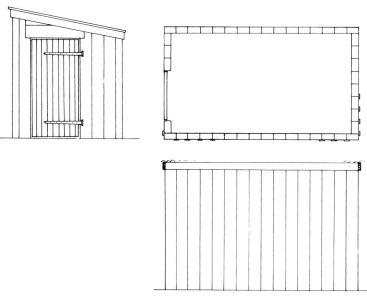

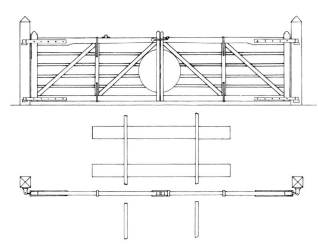

One set of crossing gates at Marston Gate, road side and plan view in 4mm:1ft scale.

Mike Crosbie

Lean-to-hut at Marston Gate, front, side and plan in 4mm:1ft scale.

Mike Crosbie

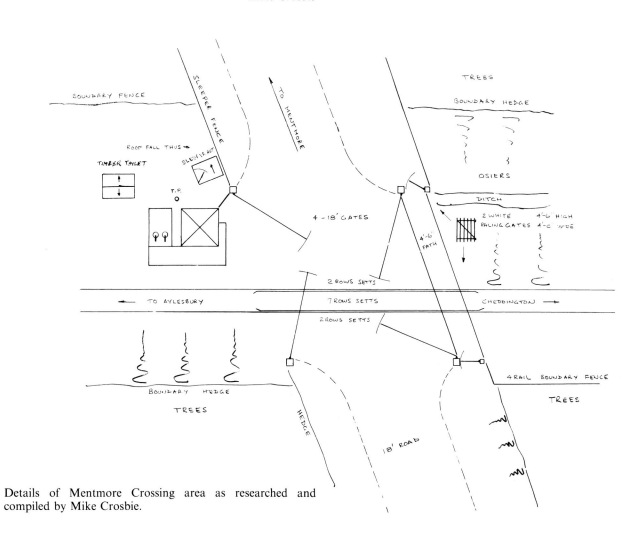

Details of Mentmore Crossing area as researched and compiled by Mike Crosbie.

Marston Gate after the end of passenger train working, although still in service for goods. The overgrown track and general appearance of an unused yard must have contrasted with the occasional visit by a 3-cylinder express passenger engine on goods trains.

Lens of Sutton

Marston Gate looking in the Cheddington direction. Jack Rogers, porter/signalman of many years, (all of them spent at this station), walks up the platform at the far end. Photograph 24th January 1953.

H.C. Casserley

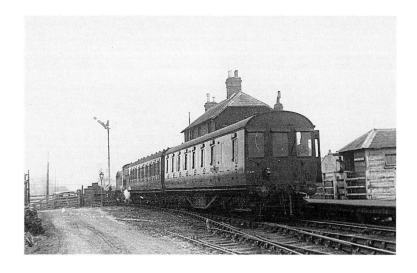

The ex-LMS push-pull set employed on the branch from 1950 on its way from Aylesbury to Cheddington. Remarkably it appears to be in the charge of an ex-Midland 2P 4-4-0. It is surprising that this method of working was not introduced earlier. Date of photograph is 24th January 1953.

H.C. Casserley

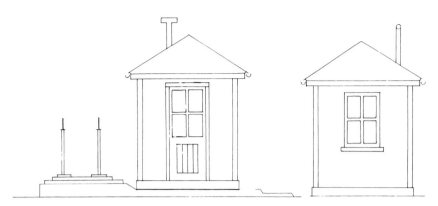

Mentmore Crossing hut front and east side in 4mm:1ft scale.
Mike Crosbie

Stephenson's original survey took the railway very close to the village of Long Marston. In actuality the route was a mile away, between this village and Wingrave.

Bucks Public Record Office

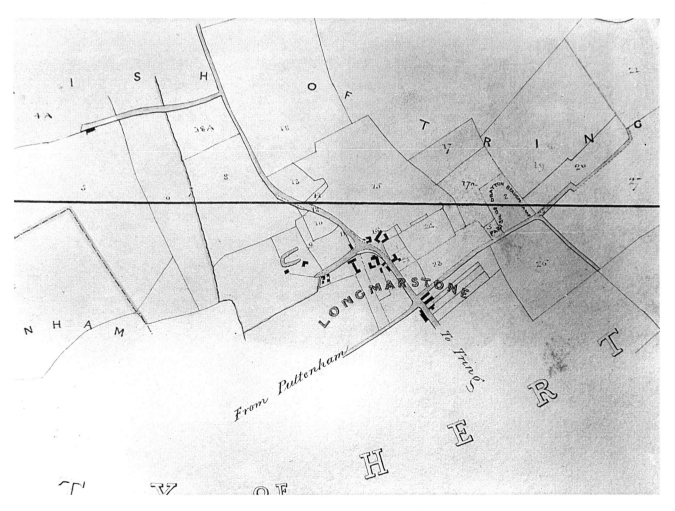

Photographs taken by the railway writer and modeller the late John Ahern, in passenger service days. It is a fascinating cameo collection of all the residual installations and devices needed to service a small country railhead. A subject of no exception when the photographs were taken but hardly existing at all nowadays.

John Ahern/Model Railway News

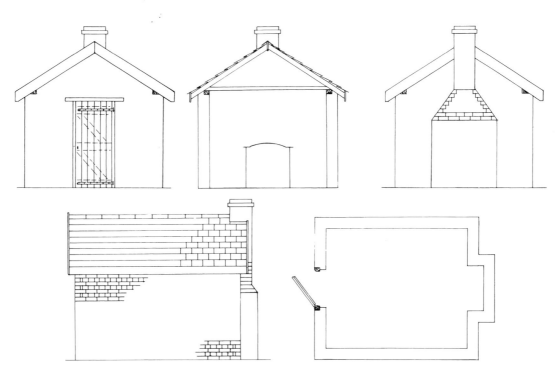

Front, back and section, side and plan view of permanent way hut No. 8, $^3/_4$ mile east of Marston Gate, drawn in 4mm:1ft scale.
Mike Crosbie

Mentmore Crossing looking from the Aylesbury side towards Cheddington, September 1957. In the distance is the fixed distant signal for Cheddington, the distant for the 'down' direction was at the end of the Cheddington platform, under the platform starter.
Geoff Williams

Staff for this modest installation was a stationmaster, the first grade for young and ambitious men of this calling to begin their ascendant career. There were also two porter/signalmen working on opposite shifts of 6am-2pm and 2pm-10pm for six days.

Goods handled besides the familiar coal, milk and cattle were supplies of chaff brought from the Aylesbury Brewery as a by-product to feed local cattle. Many carts heaped high with this cheap cattle feed would sway out of the station yard to various farms in the district.

The isolation of the station did provide a living for a local called George Paine who acquired a wagonette that could carry eight people and sundry articles of luggage between Long Marston and Wingrave, the villages immediately north and south of the line.

The crossing keeper's hut at Mentmore Crossing in 1957. Note the two-lever frame.

Geoff Williams

Mentmore Crossing from the roadside, September 1957.

Geoff Williams

Chapter 5

Cheddington

A striking view at the north end of Cheddington station with a 4-cylinder Webb Compound passing through the station. The engine would be enjoying the downhill stretch to Leighton Buzzard having worked hard up the long climb from Euston over Tring Summit. In the foreground the connecting points between the main lines and the branch platform are on the right. Of particular interest is the Saxby style signal cabin that was replaced by a large Type 5 LNWR box in 1905. *L&GRP Courtesy of David & Charles*

Opened to serve the branch as Aylesbury Railway Junction in 1839 the station was little more than a platform for changing trains. Besides Cheddington itself there is a scattering of small villages and farms. One, called Mentmore, was to become more widely known when the country house of the Rothschilds was built adjoining it in 1851.

The two platforms enclosed a pair of 'up' and 'down' lines for the main line which was supplemented with the third goods relief road in 1859. The Aylesbury line had a single connection immediately north of the station platforms.

It is interesting to contemplate why the junction was built facing north, as upon first consideration one would assume that the natural choice would be to face London. This is not quite so obvious as one might suppose, as much goods working would be expected from the north, coal from Midland collieries, and an increasing demand for this at Oxford, the hoped for eventual destination. Besides coal there would be the prospect of all manner of produce from ironworks to pottery from the industrial cornucopia centred around Birmingham with textiles from the north. From Aylesbury and district

would be the produce of intensive sheep farming wool and arable farming. Only later with the expansion of the dairy industry would that production intensify towards London. To a lesser extent the junction would be convenient for engines and stock passing from and to Wolverton.

Subsequently the station developed a degree of focal interest for local commerce, a station house was built in February 1840 and cattle docks and milk loading platforms were added. A local coal merchant, Turney, established agreement with the LNWR for a private siding and Cheddington's name appeared at last on a private owner wagon.

Another contract of 12th February 1869 with one James Copcutt of Aylesbury Gasworks was for the installation of a small gasworks at the station. "To be erected and maintained by Copcutt, gas for lighting signals and premises connected therewith, also approach roads. Gas from sulphurated hydrogen to 14 candle power. Rent for works a shilling (5p) per annum; LNWR to pay six shillings (30p) for every 1,000 cubic feet for the first year. The LNWR will allow James Copcutt first class travel between Aylesbury and

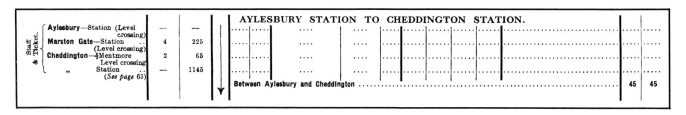

				AYLESBURY STATION TO CHEDDINGTON STATION.								
Staff & Ticket.	Aylesbury—Station (Level crossing)	---	—		....	....	....	....	....	....			....
	Marston Gate—Station .. (Level crossing)	4	225		....	....	....	....	....	....			....
	Cheddington—Mentmore Level crossing	2	65		....	....	....	....	....	....			....
	„ Station .. (See page 63)	—	1145		....	....	....	....	....	....			....
				Between Aylesbury and Cheddington						45	45	

Working Appendix instructions in 1937.

Cyril Gibbins' Collection

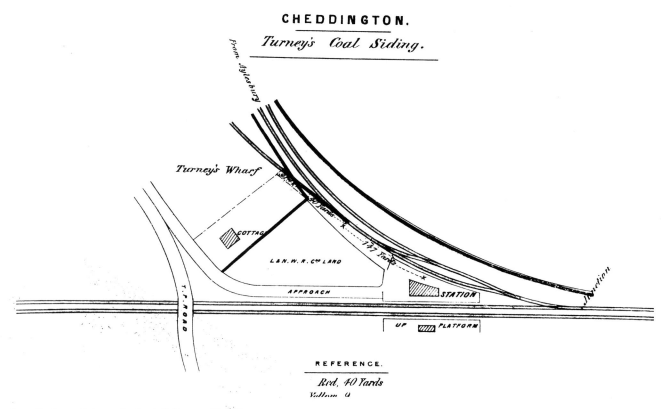

Installation of Turney's Coal Siding at Cheddington.

John Pritchett Collection

Cheddington free during construction. His workmen to be allowed the same concession in second class. Also free cartage of all necessary materials and tools. Agreement to include the distant signals for Cheddington and the signal box. Signed James Blenkinsop, Euston."

Judging by the only photograph of the first station, the gasworks is visible, as are the lamps on the platform, therefore it can be assumed that the contract was enacted. In the case of the signalling installations this may well have been experimental. Certainly after all signalling had been renewed in the 1880s the process of illumination was the conventional oil lamp. A letter to the Board by F.W. Webb on 23rd September 1881 contains a further reference to it. "... and as a result of

a defunct agreement the plant is entirely in the hands of the LNWR."

Signalman Len Kinchens of the Cheddington box remembers that the gas producing equipment was converted in the 1930s to a petrol engine generator with a huge rotating fan on it. There were two pillars with a weight suspended between them which slowly came down but if it was allowed to touch the ground the gas would go out. The Rosebery Arms was also supplied and the company employed the village blacksmith to maintain the system.

Understandably the area around Cheddington became influenced significantly by the decision of Mayer Amschel Rothschild to build the elaborate edifice of Mentmore Towers nearby, designed by Paxton, only a year after his celebrated palace of glass in Hyde Park –

Although the station is looking its years in this picture it remains tidy in appearance. Early days of British Railways on the 4th August 1949 with rebuilt 'Patriot' class No.45540 *Sir Robert Turnbull* waiting in the 'down' fast. Signals at the end of the branch line platform are the platform starter and the distant for Mentmore Crossing.

H.C. Casserley

Simmering patiently in the branch line platform is the assembly of humble tank engine and two coaches, waiting to return to Aylesbury with the evening train. The contrast between this train and those of the main line platforms typifies the age of change that could prove to be a delectation in itself. The engine is ex-LNWR Webb 1P class 2-4-2 tank No.46666 on 4th August 1949.

H.C. Casserley

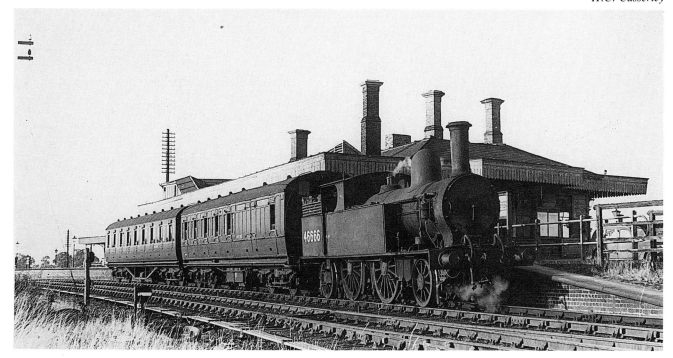

CHEDDINGTON

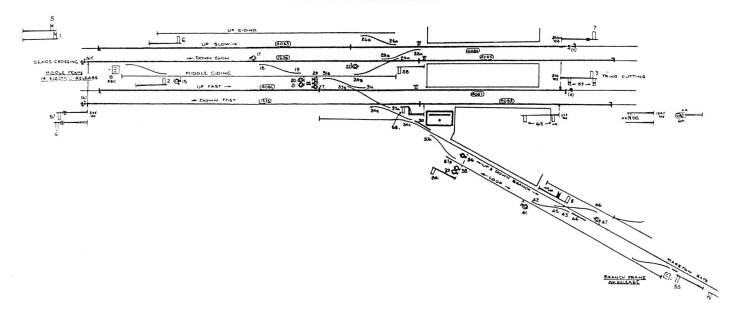

Cheddington as rebuilt for 25kv electrification but still with mechanical signalling. The branch was operated as a goods only line at this time.

G.K. Fox Collection

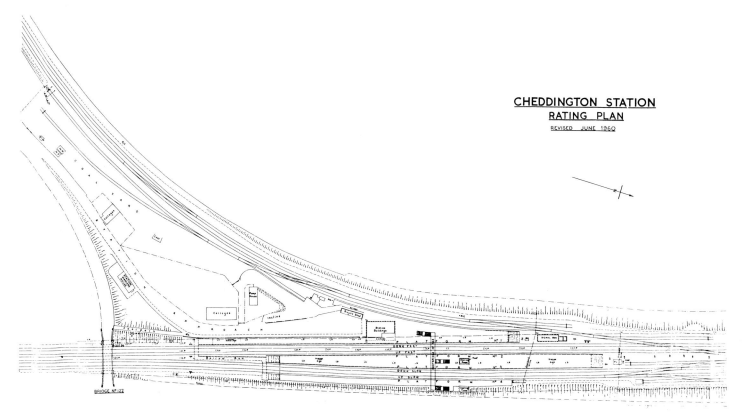

CHEDDINGTON STATION
RATING PLAN
REVISED JUNE 1960

Cheddington in 1888 in its fullest form which is how it remained until the drastic changes of the late 1950s and 1960s wrought by rebuilding and electrification of the signalling.

Ordnance Survey

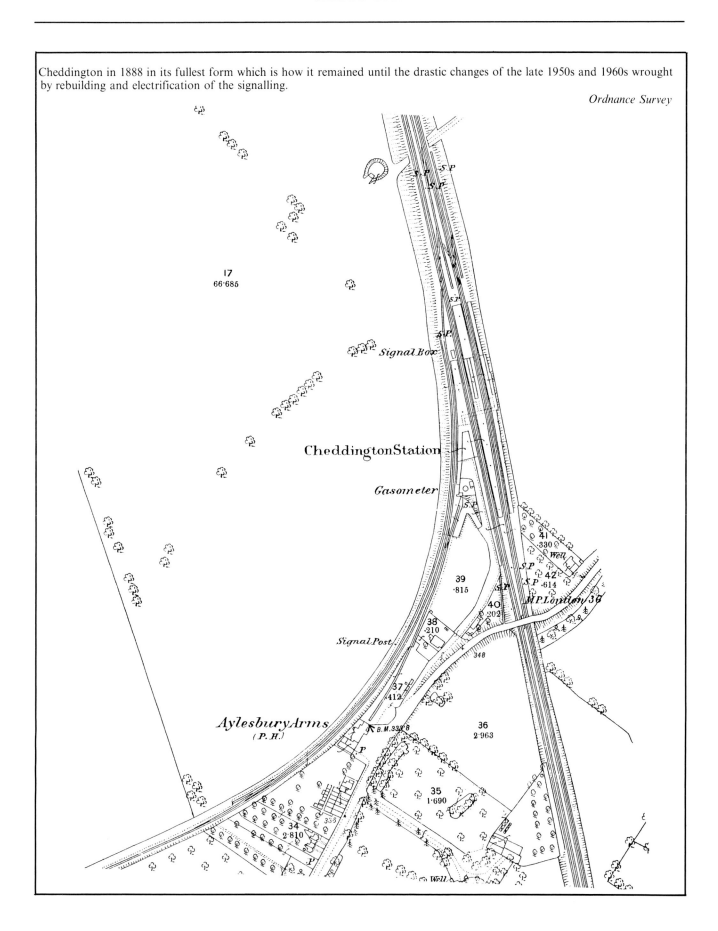

17
66·685

Signal Box

Cheddington Station

Gasometer

S.P

41
·330

Well

39
·815

42
·614

40
202

M.P. London 36

38
·210

Signal Post

348

37
·412

Aylesbury Arms
(P.H.)

B.M. 333·8

P

36
2·963

35
1·690

356

34
2·810

P

Well

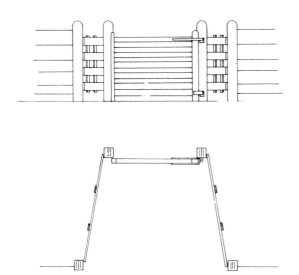

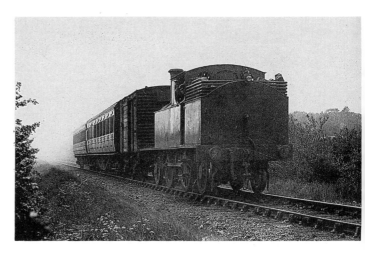

Unusual occupation crossing gate design near Cheddington.
Drawn in 4mm:1ft scale.

Mike Crosbie

The last summer before the second World War No.6687 nears
Cheddington from Aylesbury with the 2.38pm train on 30th
May 1939.

LCGB Ken Nunn Collection

The Great Exhibition building. The Rothschilds
favoured the area around Aylesbury, Anthony bought a
house at Aston Clinton, Lionel bought Halton and
farms at Hulcott and Bierton as well as Tring Park, with
other Rothschild Houses at Eythrope and Waddesdon.
Anthony was Aylesbury's M.P. in 1867.

Their style cut across traditional lordly isolation with
incidental but humane practices like keeping all their
labourers employed during the winter. Neither did they
care to suffer their large houses but relished the
trappings of wealth by having hot water and central
heating pipes. Also in summer artificial ventilation, or
the modern term – air conditioning.

Keen on horses they enjoyed equestrian meets and
loved hunting in the Vale of Aylesbury. The rows of
gleaming horse boxes at Cheddington station were often
placed along the siding beside the branch.

The marriage of Hannah Rothschild to Lord
Rosebery meant that Mentmore was newly owned and
after her death in 1890 it remained in that family until
1977 when the executors of the 6th Earl of Rosebery
disposed of the house and its contents. At the time of
writing it belongs to 'The World Government' with its
head, the mystic Maharishi Mahesh Yogi.

In the early 1870s came the quadrupling of the
LNWR main line and the drastic changes necessary.
Cheddington was totally re-built and the branch rails
re-aligned. Imposing long platforms to accept the

developing need for long trains were spanned by a 42ft
9in footbridge supported on cast iron columns and
brackets. The station buildings took on what became a
form of corporate style of the LNWR, modular timber
structures under wide flat awnings.

A further development of trade in a considerable way
was the burgeoning fruit growing interests of the area.
Enormous quantities of baskets would be brought from
London to Cheddington spilling over the goods yard
area. They were filled from the nearby orchards of
plums, damsons and a special damson for producing
prunes. The growers did complain rather sourly that the
railway company would never reduce their rates whether
the prices were 16s 0d (80p) or 6d (2^1/2p) per flat,
therefore the growers had to balance their output at a
profitable level. Nevertheless it was by no means
exceptional in the season for ten to fifteen tons of fruit to
be despatched from Cheddington each day.

To haul them were the gleaming black inspirations of
Crewe works which by 1923 became sullied by the
reddening hue of Derby with the formation of the
London Midland & Scottish Railway.

By the time the 4-4-0 Compounds and 4-6-0 'Royal
Scots' had themselves been superseded by the mighty
Pacific classes, a memory of the LNWR lingered in the
form of "The Corridor" train curiously retitled the
"Mid-Day Scot".

Chapter 6

Engines and Rolling Stock

Having brought in the 1.00pm train from Aylesbury on 12th August 1950 an ageing ex-LNWR tank No.46601 pauses at Cheddington before returning with the 1.25pm.

LCGB Ken Nunn Collection

After the displacement of the two Bury engines the branch was owned and operated by the LNWR with its engines and rolling stock. During the late 1840s and early 1850s the station called 'Bletchley and Fenny Stratford', 47 miles from Euston was developing significantly. This was as a result of the opening of the line to Bedford in 1846 and another line to Oxford in 1851. Also in 1850 a branch from the Oxford line near Claydon to Banbury was built and opened. The Oxford line in effect stole the original colours of the Aylesbury Railway intentions.

The village of Bletchley grew to become a major railway centre, the population increasing with almost totally railway personnel, to 4,000 inhabitants.

Bletchley shed became divisional headquarters No.3 after Camden No.1 and Watford No.2. Its motive power and carriage stock to supply the branches: Aylesbury (1839), Bedford (1846), Leighton Buzzard (1848), Banbury (1850), Oxford (1851), Cambridge (1862) and Newport Pagnell (1866). At the end of each of these branches was a sub-shed.

The area of Bletchley's control stretched from just north of Tring to a point just south of Roade, a distance of some 28 miles, added to this was 142 miles of branch line track.

The shed was a familiar double-hipped roof design sprouting numerous ventilation flues, it was 250ft long by 100ft wide enclosing six roads which could accommodate 24 tender engines or 36 tank engines. It replaced an original shed of timber and galvanised iron which was blown down in 1876. Presumably the new shed was built shortly after a great deal of rebuilding took place in the early eighties.

For motive power Bletchley was of course allocated to supply the power needs of the area, 46 engines at Bletchley (1910) itself with a further 14 at the outstations, the lions share of these would probably be at Oxford which was the largest of these.

In 1910 there were 240 personnel, footplate and various shed grades that operated an engine allocation of: 4 'Precursors' (Whale); several eight-coupled goods engines three of which were compound goods engines; 6

Ex-LNWR 2-4-2T No.6687 leaving Cheddington on 30th May 1939 with the 3.25pm working.

LCGB Ken Nunn Collection

0-6-0 Coal engines; 13 18″ Goods engines ("Cauli-flowers"); 6 5ft 6in 2-4-2 tank engines; 4 shunting engines and several 'Precedent' and 'Waterloo' class 2-4-0s. Two units of Whale/Parke steam railmotors arrived in 1905 along with a spare engine unit. There was always a duty engine held in steam continuously for main line relief and this was usually one of three four-cylinder compounds which ostensibly should be filling its time with shunting duties.

During the 1930s after the formation of the London Midland & Scottish Railway, six Aspinall 0-6-0 goods engines were seconded from their ex-Lancashire & Yorkshire haunts to work Bletchley diagrams. Their displacement was said to be due to falling requirements in the North West because of the slump in the cotton industry. Nicknamed "Gracie Fields" by Bletchley men they did not remain isolated exiles for long as they were joined by a number of LYR 'Saddletank' 0-6-0 shunting engines utilised in the Bletchley marshalling yard. These led largely inglorious lives clanking back and forth amongst acres of wagons and for this purpose they were well received by the Bletchley footplate staff. With the exigencies of wartime the Bletchley depot alone was catering for 67 engines and manned by 600 personnel.

Insomuch as the branch is concerned early locomotives after the Bury engines are difficult to be precise about. A memorandum from the sub-committee of the Southern Division to the Locomotive Superintendent J.E. McConnell at Wolverton to remove the heavy engines from the branch could be referring to the new 0-6-0 goods engine, or to the Stephenson long boilered

engines that were being utilised on the branches at that time.

The first photographic evidence for the engines used is of Cheddington station c1874 showing a McConnell engine standing at the branch platform with four-wheel stock. One occupant of the branch workings is believed to have been No. 263 *Pheasant* of the 'Samson' class in the early 1890s.

A seven mile branch working from a junction station was bound to become the metier of tank engine working and some developments of the tank engine construction took place mid-century. Further the batches of 2-4-0, 2-4-2 and 0-6-2s, from 1881, started to roll out of Crewe in the 1870s. Certainly the Webb 1P 5ft 6in (1890) version and the 0-6-2 'Coal' tanks are believed to have taken occupancy on the branch from their inception and photographic evidence supports their use up until the early 1950s. In LMS days it is understood ex-LNWR "Watford" tanks ran the service.

With the formation of British Railways in 1948 brand new Ivatt 2-6-2 tanks operated the service, particularly No.41275. About twelve months later Aylesbury shed effectively closed when the engines for passenger work were stabled and operated from Leighton Buzzard shed in 1950, with Leighton men. Last thing at night the locomotive would leave the stock at Aylesbury and run light back to Leighton, returning light the following morning.

This displacement of personnel, with the options of jobs elsewhere or leaving altogether, sent drivers and firemen over to the Met. & GCR Joint by now called

Aylesbury Town. The guards had left earlier when the push-pull working was introduced and had gone to work on main line trains which must have been quite a drastic change from this ambling branch line. The situation with the Leighton men did not continue very long for only three years later, on the 2nd February 1953 the passenger service of the Aylesbury branch was discontinued.

The last train ceremony was not without sentiment, 2-4-2 tank No.46601 was brought back to run it and one of the guards, George Thorn took a breather from his main line duties to take his last trip on a branch he had known for so long. It was a fitting tribute to the 63 year old engine which by the end of the year would itself be in the breaker's yard.

A Webb Coal tank was not denied the opportunity to pay its final respects by courtesy of the Locomotive Club of Great Britain who booked a special with No.58887 along the branch on the 10th October 1954. This engine was withdrawn in the following April.

Goods working on the Aylesbury branch continued for a further ten years with one train a day, keenly made use of by the Aylesbury businesses. This train was handled by a mixture of engines which depended either on haulage requirements or more likely availability. Standard profiles for the trip were the ex-LNWR eight-coupled types which in their final form were known collectively as 'Super Ds' which were often rostered with ex-Midland 4F 0-6-0 types. The alternative assortment included Stanier 2-6-0 tender engines, Hughes/Fowler 2-6-0 tender engines known as "Crabs", some "Black Fives" and occasionally members of the three-cylinder classes Nos 45511 *Isle of Man* and 45722 *Defence* being noted. There is no evidence to suggest that a diesel locomotive had ventured thus far.

On 2nd December 1963 the echoes of exhausting steam, shouting men and clatter of recalcitrant goods wagons left the scene forever, indeed it would only be a matter of five years before it had left the entire system. In view of the weight of competition both from the other station and road transport, not to mention the fury of motorists at Park Street crossing, it showed remarkable resilience in lasting as long as it did.

Evidently from the photograph on page 86 of the train at Cheddington, early LNWR four-wheel stock was used on the branch, and this would in all probability, have continued for many years, possibly up to the last decade of the 19th century. The displacement of six-wheel stock from main line running with the advent of radial and bogie stock, which was also introduced on the Oxford to Cambridge route, would have displaced them to the branches.

It appears that two sets of six-wheel coaches operated on the branch, coaches being maintained in fixed sets at the Bletchley depot. Each set consisted of three coaches in each, the outer pair braked with the guards

On 17th June 1950 2-6-0 No.43001 makes the leisurely trip down from Bletchley with the 2.05pm Aylesbury goods near Mentmore Crossing. Although not quite three years old these engines were derided by Bletchley men as lacking in pulling power, and certainly not considered to be up to the ex-Midland 4Fs they were intended to replace. Later modifications like conversions to single chimney rectified this to some degree in later years. The goods train is of course a daily antiquity on the branch and continued long after the passenger service ceased, when the spaciousness evident on this photograph became largely overgrown.

LCGB Ken Nunn Collection

compartment, probably 30ft 6in thirds and the centre vehicle possibly a 32ft 1st, 3rd and two 2nds. Another composite was held in reserve at Cheddington for use on market day.

From the early days of the LMS the sets used on the line consisted of two bogie coaches, these often including enduring ex-LNWR stock.

For a few months in 1950 push-pull working was introduced on the branch but this appears to have been a belated introduction of that method of working.

Appropriate to the needs of a local branch the Aylesbury line accommodated a multiplicity of purposes for its goods customers, from the early unsprung, dumb-buffered trucks with their coal, sheep, hay fodder and manure assembled ad hoc in any train as required, in the daily goods plodding its seven miles back and forth after collecting and despatching its allocation at Cheddington. Besides the horse boxes and cattle wagons of later more distinctive development were the six-wheel ventilated milk vans supported by 45ft clerestory bogie vehicles for Nestlés supplies, with oil tank wagons for the petrol depots and timber wagons for Richards the local timber merchant.

Pre-eminently **LNWR** with a long train and a shiny black engine at the head, No.1105 *Hercules* a 'Precedent' class 2-4-0 braces itself for Tring Summit before the run to Euston. The train of non-corridor stock appears to be having a coach detached from the rear.
L&GRP Courtesy of David & Charles

Near Mentmore Crossing the 2.20pm (Saturdays only) has just left Cheddington on the 17th June 1950. Evidently rostered with one of the push-pull units but obviously not working as such.
LCGB Ken Nunn Collection

Chapter 7

Recollections of the Line

Station staff assemble in the front of the 64 lever signalbox at Cheddington in 1922 in this now faded photograph. The box spanned a block section between Sear's Crossing (north) and Tring Cutting (south). A good example of the intensity of railway labour is seen here with the Stationmaster accompanied by three shift foremen each supervising four porters beneath them on each shift. Also there were three signalmen operating the box on a 24-hour three-shift system.

Len Kinchens' Collection

An essential contribution to historical studies is the first hand accounts of events, drawn from direct personal experience. Although memory can be uncertain, in the case of railwaymen whose occupations were literally governed by regulations and the necessity of good timekeeping, experiences tend to be recalled by the modification or alteration of routine. It is therefore extremely useful to hear what men and women can relate directly from their working lives although, there are few railwaymen around now who can recall life with the pre-Grouping companies. In recognition of this it is doubly essential to accumulate what knowledge is still available.

R.H. Thompkins who, at the time of writing, was 87 years of age, recollects his early railway career at Cheddington when he was a junior booking clerk. After his first twelve months as a clerk at Euston in 1913 he went to Leighton Buzzard in 1916. Shortly afterwards he went to Cheddington also working as a relief at Aylesbury station. In his days there was plenty of activity to keep him occupied. The dairy production of the district was an important share of consignments. All the milk collected at Marston Gate station was brought to Aylesbury works of Nestlés, impressive if one realises

that something close to the amount of fifty churns a day were being loaded from that station, often filling the guards' sections at each end of the train. On Wednesdays the 9 o'clock passenger train ex-Cheddington brought cattle from that station and from Marston Gate to Aylesbury market. If just cows it would be one van, while sheep too would be provided with an extra van. Dominion Dairy in Aylesbury produced large quantities of butter in 14lb boxes which filled many vans.

Goods for Aylesbury were always put in the middle siding at Cheddington to be collected by the continuing stream of freights moving north and south, branch loads were usually re-sorted at Bletchley.

A regular goods consignment were wagons called 'London Sweepings' which were the horse droppings of the streets of London. Farmers at Cheddington and Marston would compete keenly to get a load from these wagons which were rationed to the district at about ten wagons a week. One must bear in mind the successful fruit orchards of the district.

Amongst livestock were the stud mares to be sired at the Rosebery Stables. Mr. Thompkins remembers many of them coming to Cheddington via Verney Junction. They were in gleaming horse boxes with various family

Staff of Cheddington station about 1922. The war veteran seated on the left in trilby hat was Harry Howkins. Being disabled he was reinstated on the railway as crossing keeper which was usual practice for ex-servicemen. He was the keeper at Mentmore Crossing. The man sitting on the Stationmaster's right was Joe Missenden, one of five brothers of a railway family. He served at nearly all the stations along the Oxford to Cambridge route besides Cheddington and Aylesbury. As goods clerk he was the very last employee at Aylesbury station and handed over the keys etc. to the stationmaster of Aylesbury Town station on the very last day.

Len Kinchens

Very neat and businesslike the Cheddington box interior circa 1955. A further ten years would see its end with the introduction of the Bletchley panel box which controlled a 22 mile section from just north of Castlethorpe to Tring Cutting, a few miles south of Cheddington.

Geoff Williams

Cheddington station staff in 1911. Third from the left standing is believed to be the Aylesbury branch guard, whilst his driver and fireman are third and fourth from the right. Sadly, fireman Missenden, who was one of several brothers who were all railway employees in the area, was killed in the First World War. Ironically another brother who was porter at the station in 1911 was the last railway employee at Aylesbury in 1963 when be personally closed the goods depot and turned the key for the last time. The man in the very wide hat seated on the left, eventually became stationmaster at Liverpool Lime Street.

Len Kinchen's Collection

names and crests adorning the fine handiwork of the coach builders' craft. After producing foals they left for Verney Junction or Bletchley destined sometimes for the north of Scotland.

Still on the subject of horses, many working horses were brought from Euston to Cheddington station, 16 to 30 at a time. They were grazed in the fields adjoining Putnam Old Rectory. The reason why they came was due to Mr H. Turner being the horse superintendent of the LNWR who had land there and brought the horses from their labours to be rested for one month at a time.

Between Marston Gate and Cheddington was the crossing for the driveway to Mentmore Towers, which was controlled by two men on two shifts, 6am until 2pm and 2pm until 10pm. One of the men, Harry Barnfather, had only one leg; it was often the case that a man sustaining injuries on another part of the company's system would be found easier employment like this. Besides the gate they had a 'home' signal on the 'up' side

whilst on the 'down' there was one distant signal between Mentmore Crossing and Cheddington. The crossing had a three-lever frame and a gate hut containing communication instruments.

During the pre-Grouping era it was usual for small stations to carry the first grade of station master, after that time these stations were in many cases reduced to one man operation which would be porter-in-charge. Mr Joseph Millar was the last man to carry the rank of station master at Marston Gate and it is with indebtedness to his daughter, Mrs McLees, that this account of life at the station in 1922 to 1926 can be described.

Joseph Millar started as a booking clerk at Bletchley station in 1915 until he was called up for service in the Royal Engineers. He returned to this post in 1919 but was ambitious enough to gain promotion to Marston Gate in 1922. It was not a move that the young family cherished at first. They arrived one morning on a train

One of the principal customers at Cheddington was Turney's coal yard. This had its own private siding shown here with one of the Turney horse drawn coal carts well stocked for its rounds in the locality. Mrs Turney was the landlady of the Rosebery Hotel. The South Eastern & Chatham Railway coal wagon must have travelled well from the Kent coalfields. The assembly of vans behind probably concern the piles of fruit baskets on the right. The Cheddington area was famous for its damson and prune orchards.

Len Kinchens

Panoramic view of the branch line platform on the right with the 'up' and 'down' fast lines on the left. A little of the branch line engine can be seen to the right of the coaches as it runs round its train for the return trip. This view is believed to be in the late 1920s.

L&GRP Courtesy of David & Charles

Days of plenitude in the yard at Cheddington as fruit baskets arrive for the nearby orchards of damsons and prunes in 1922. In the distance are the fog cottages where three linemen or gangers used to live. The middle house in the row had an alarm bell that could be activated by the signalman in the event of thickening fog. The man answering the alarm would inform the two other occupants on each side and they would report for duty as fogmen placing detonators and waving lamps by the lineside.

Len Kinchens' Collection

The branch line train leaving Cheddington, with the end stop of the long siding just visible on the left. This photograph taken on the 27th August 1938.

J.P. Mullett

Early Cheddington station photograph, taken between the completion of the gas lighting contract of 1870, as the lamps are on the station buildings, and the quadrupling of the line from Euston to Bletchley in 1876. Of particular note is the Saxby style signal box and the slotted post semaphores, and according to the stipulation of the contract these too had gas lighting. The third line on the right was the additional goods relief line between Bletchley and Primrose Hill. Initially for goods trains but, as can be seen by the arrangement of the platform fencing on the 'up' side it was used to supplement paths for passenger trains. The engine, which can just be seen, on the branch line train left, looks like a McConnell 2-2-2 with four-wheel stock. Extensive rebuilding with four tracks later was to change the station completely.

M.D. Grant Collection

ahead of their belongings that were loaded onto a train to arrive in the afternoon, which meant that before they could be shunted into the siding they would have to pass straight by them and go to Aylesbury, first to be shunted into the siding from an 'up' facing train.

As a young girl Mrs McLees recalls that the station seemed cold and empty, although a fire could be lit and Mrs Millar made do for refreshment, by brewing tea on the fire and cutting food on the high mantle shelf above it. The Millar family soon made the station a pleasant home and the children enjoyed their life there with regular trains and friendly railway staff and passengers. It all made a deep impression on her brother Harold who sought employment on the railway as soon as he came of working age. He went to work on another branch in the Bletchley control area, the one from Wolverton to Newport Pagnell.

Besides himself Mr Millar had two porter/signalmen working early and late shifts to keep the station open from six in the morning to ten at night. One of these men, both of whom lived in the village, was Jack Rogers who deserves special mention because he served all of his railway career at Marston Gate, from 1920 until closure

in 1963. Although Mr Millar tried to encourage Jack to try for promotional posting elsewhere on the company's system Jack would have none of it.

Not so Mr Millar who, with a young family to bring up, and little to restrain his ambition, (even the charms of Marston Gate) applied for better positions subsequently, first in 1926 at Bricket Wood which also included responsibility for nearby Park Street. During his time there he was called upon to handle many long excursion trains. Then in 1931 he moved the family to Rainham, also covering Dagenham Docks. Traffic here was intense with the burgeoning Ford Motor Works. Finally they moved to Harrow & Wealdstone from whence he retired in 1951. Thankfully before one of Britain's worst railway disasters in 1952.

During the time at Marston Gate the significant traffic, beside passenger trains and coal, was the milk, cattle and grain. The grain being the chaff of barley used by Aylesbury Brewery and prized by local farmers for cattle feed. On Wednesday market days the Edmondson ticket punch would have its busiest morning, continually thumping as farmers congregated on the station in their best tweeds bound for Aylesbury cattle market, not to mention the hostelries of that town.

Distinctly 1930's vintage as this 'up' express hammers through Cheddington behind the imposing lines of the premier engine of the 'Royal Scot' class No.46100, complete with Stanier tender. She would be feeling the effects now of the 1 in 333 for six miles to Tring Summit. The tank engine of that same designer on the right is probably on the 'down' slow from Euston to Bletchley. Date of photograph, 23rd July 1938. *J.P. Mullett*

The large stone blocks of the milk loading dock suggest that it originates from the earliest days of the station. An interesting comparison can be made between the traditional and the emerging change in transport vehicles, with the gig and the solid tyred lorry. *M.D. Grant Collection*

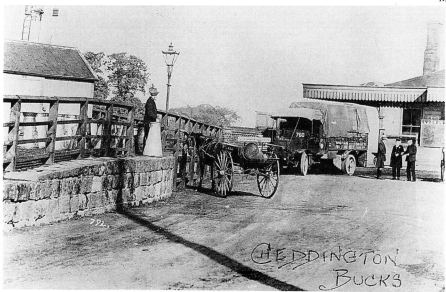

An irritating feature of the locality was Langdale Brook which passed under the road between the station and Marston village. In a very wet season this was likely to flood over the road and build up a very large volume of water cutting the station off from the village.

A Mrs Wilkins of Wingrave was another user of Marston Gate station in the 1930s, when she worked at a clothing works at Berkhamsted. Her ticket, renewable each month cost 12s 6d (62¹/₂p). She remembered the period shortly after Mr Millar left and Jack Rogers moved into the station house. His opposite shift colleague, Charlie Mason, lived in Long Marston, and there were then only two men operating the station. The local coalman Jack Lee, lived in a house close to the station and had his coal drops in the station yard. She remembered that milk leaving the station was stood on a special milk platform close to the ticket office.

Cheddington in the 1930s with the branch line train possibly waiting its connection, not yet having run-round for its return journey. The soot blackened footbridge expresses mindfully that enginemen would certainly be 'winding it up' at this point to ensure an effective run over Tring Summit. At 420ft above sea level this is the highest point of the London & Birmingham part of the main line.

J.P. Mullett

Exemplary presentation from the Gloucester Railway Carriage & Wagon Co. Turney's new wagon in red lead, white letters shaded black.

Historical Model Railway Society

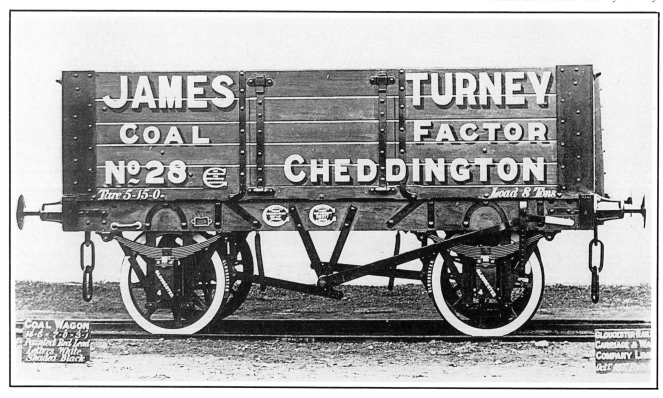

A platform only of weeds as 4F class 0-6-0 No.44364 wanders into the once-passenger area of the station having brought in the daily goods train. The only reason for it to enter this melancholy area was to use the water column. The day is 28th November 1960 and by now this single daily working was just about keeping the line from being choked by nature's attempts to conceal it.

Geoff Williams

The additional muscle and braking power of the 2-6-2 tanks enabled goods working to be supplemented with that curiosity of the branch line era, the passenger/goods push-pull train. Locomotive No.41275 has arrived with this assembly in 1950 and will presumably detach from the coaches and take the goods train to the yard. On the platform is guard Dick Ewers and fireman Wesley Robins.

L & GRP Courtesy David & Charles

One of the personal services that the line catered for its passengers, was for a Mrs French who lived at Betlow Farm which was close by the line, two miles from Cheddington. The train often stopped to pick her up or let her off, almost at her front door!

During the Second World War the local people became nervous of travelling on the railway, especially after a bomb or landmine exploded in a field close to Marston Gate station. For people working at the clothing factory a special bus was put on that called at Wingrave and from that time on Mrs French ceased to use the railway. Even with petrol rationing after the war, bus competition remained a threat to the railway.

Driver Arthur Waller is now over 90 years of age and still living in Aylesbury, one of the few locomotive drivers that can still talk about life under the LNWR. He started work on the railway in 1914 at Bletchley as a cleaner in the shed. Then took the rough job of coal boy filling tenders. After being promoted to the drier occupation of storeman he joined the army in 1917. Upon demob in 1919 he returned to Bletchley to take up

his job as a fireman at Banbury shed, a sub-depot of Bletchley. This was in the days when that branch was operated by a single engine with two 'sets' of men. Each night the engines would be changed over at Brackley by changing crews between the goods train and the passenger train. In the early days the Ramsbottom DX class 0-6-0s were used, but he only remembered the Webb 18in goods 0-6-0s.

Mr Waller worked the Banbury branch for many years, later as a driver and did not start on the Aylesbury branch until 3rd March 1938. He operated the branch with another driver, two firemen and two guards, George Thorn and Dick Ewers. He confirms the method of gravity shunting the coaches was common practice at that time, avoiding the need for using the loop.

Driver Waller's engine on the branch was No. 6601, Webb 2-4-2T which can be seen in numerous photographs in this book.

The Aylesbury station area amounted to a small railway community. Arthur lived in a house close to the

Not a very clear print but a rarity in photographing a large 4-6-0 on the branch in passenger working days. The Black 5 No.45405 is visiting with a football excursion in the early 1950s. Jack Turner, fireman and guard George Thorn are on the footplate whilst driver Arthur Waller is standing on the platform.

Jack Turner

For the last three years of the passenger service the line saw brand new locomotives working from Leighton Buzzard Shed. Ivatt 2-6-2 tank No.41275 began her years on this duty and is seen here on 20th July 1951 at Cheddington.

T.J. Edgington

A sentimental journey for ex-LNWR 2-4-2 tank No.46601. The prodigal load of five coaches would awaken thoughts of pre-1923 for anything close to that kind of load on the branch. In this case the finalé with the last passenger train on 2nd February 1953.

Bucks Free Press

Well removed from the site of the signal box at Aylesbury the station frame that operated the points and signals in the immediate vicinity, after release from the box. The young man standing before them is Peter Williams, son of Geoff Williams who visited the station many times to collect data for his famous 4mm scale model of the station and Dropshort Crossing.   *Geoff Williams*

Grossly foreshortened by five bays in LMS days this view of the Aylesbury LNWR steam shed on the 28th November 1960 shows it rather forlorn and vandalised. The remarkable length of this single road shed suggests that from its inception it could have been intended to hold the entire branch train, which would have been possible at that time (1845).   *Geoff Williams*

A 'raft' of mineral wagons, as the locomen liked to call them, stand alongside the bare platform. At this time the station buildings were used as provender stores, and by a local wine and spirit dealer.

Lens of Sutton

Grassy rails and weeds in wheels of the old LMS horse drawn cart rusting alongside each other on the 14th September 1963, four months before total closure.

R.M. Casserley

crossing at No. 77 Park Street with other footplatemen living close by, with one lodging with him. The two signalmen for the station lived in the cottages next to the signalbox. His brother William Waller was further down the line manning Mentmore Crossing.

Arthur Waller vividly recounted the wartime risks at Aylesbury, in particular the night the shed was damaged.

"It was in the summer twilight and we had just brought our last train in and run the engine into the shed, when my mate turns to me and says, "Here the beggers come Arthur!", and a landmine drops with a huge explosion, flying glass, smoke and dirt everywhere. Course, we all just left the engine and run like hell, my mate and me and a chap that we brought up on the last train from Marston Gate. He stayed with the engine all night leaving it on the brew until morning when we could drive straight out. Do you know that 'all clear' didn't go until three in the morning so we all crept back, floor was thick with glass and there she was simmering with just a teaspoonful of water in the bottom of the gauge glass. We just about got some into her in time – if that 'all clear' hadn't come in time we would have lost here to the plug. It was shortly after that that the LMS came and demolished half the shed and put longer draughting flues on the chimneys.

Mentmore was the place though for pheasants – at the crossing. One night I went up with the 6.30am from here and just before we got to Mentmore, travelling about forty miles an hour, I hit a cock pheasant, wallop! Down he went. So when we got into Cheddington I said to my mate that we had just hit a pheasant and I'm going to have that, because we had half an hour wait in Cheddington. It was about a mile or so back to where I hit him and in the distance I could see him. Crossing keeper gave me a funny look walking back down the line. I eventually came to a few feet of him and the begger flew off, I'd only stunned him!

They brought a push-pull on the line towards the end of my time which did away with guards, although you had to have a 'passed' fireman to operate this train.

When we had to hand the line over to Leighton Buzzard men to be worked from there we were transferred over the Met. & GCR Joint and I was out on the Great Western link so I had to work trains from Aylesbury to Wycombe and Paddington. I went but I was passed learning new line so I decided to pack it in.

Do you know I never liked the railway. From the start in 1914 to the day I left, I never liked it one minute. Trouble with the railways was that you were either at work or you was in bed, and sometimes you had to go away for weeks at a time."

A footplateman that started his career on the branch was Jack Turner who, in 1937, lived close to the terminus at Aylesbury. He started there as a goods clerk in 1942 which gave him first-hand knowledge of the goods workings on the line. A regular working was three vans leaving the station each morning by the 8.15am, which contained the current issue of the world famous *Reader's Digest* which was printed in the town by Hazell, Watson & Viney.

Another very important source of goods revenue were the dairy products from Dominion Dairies in Park Street. The working of the vans is interesting. The branch line train would deposit them at Cheddington in the middle siding on the main line. They would then be collected by an engine working light from Willesden to Cheddington. Thus formed the train would pick up the goods from Leighton Buzzard and continue north to do

Changes at Cheddington in April 1960. The station has been rebuilt in prospect no doubt for the coming of electrification, whilst earlier days are evoked by the signal box which closed on 3rd July 1965. With the cessation of passenger services the distant signal warning for Mentmore Crossing has been removed from beneath the platform starter. The method employed for goods trains going up the branch was for a member of the station staff to cycle to Mentmore crossing gates whilst the train waited in the station. An excellent view of the LNWR loading gauge.

Geoff Williams

the same at Bletchley. The final section of the journey would take the train on to Northampton where it was remarshalled for its final destination – Crewe.

Amongst Jack's duties were taking the wagon numbers to be telephoned through to Bletchley and making arrangements with local coal merchants regarding their deliveries. The gasworks had 40 wagons each day whilst other merchants collectively would have had 20 wagons – a useful 60 wagon train to be turned round each day. Amongst this would follow trains of cattle and general merchandise with a preponderence of fruit after the war, especially bananas. Another heavy user of the branch was the large depot of YCL (British Yeast) that was situated in the town. Cleveland Oil had their depot near the entrance to the goods yard and the appearance of oil tank wagons on the branch on a regular basis was to supply their requirements.

In 1948 Jack decided that the grittier solvency of oil and water was more interesting than paper and ink and left the smooth walnut-topped desk for the rigours of the footplate. It was a move he never regretted.

The number of men based at Aylesbury loco shed in 1937 was two drivers and three firemen, one being a passed fireman who sometimes took a turn on driving. After the day's running the fire on the engine was not entirely dropped but would be kept simmering in the shed under the watchful eye of one of the firemen that would take their turns. This must have been a lonely, almost eerie night shift, alone in the huge single road shed that would dwarf the engine, let alone a person. It would be his job to make sure that the engine was coaled and watered ready to start the day's work.

The men on the line much preferred a tank locomotive for the week's duties which was certainly not always the

case either in LMS or British Railways days. The reason in particular for the preference was to do with coaling the engine. Loco coal wagons were stored on the siding at Stocklake and when this was needed the engine would run back up the line to collect it and bring it down to the shed. The usual method of coaling was by shovel over the end of the wagon and back of the bunker. With a tender engine this could not be done as the distance to the coal rails was beyond the water filling cap, consequently a tender engine had to be coaled from the rails alongside, which precluded the man in charge of this duty from carrying it out inside the shed. The advantage of doing this in shelter could not be overstated in cold wind and freezing rain.

On the lighter side Jack remembers the personal touches of the local railways so vividly, such as bringing the fish and chips from Aylesbury to Cheddington on the last train, kept warm on the 'mantlepiece' – the back plate of the locomotive firebox.

During a return trip from Cheddington with a Webb Coal tank a minor blow-back was experienced and the engine came to a stall. This was in open country still miles from Aylesbury. Jack then proceeded to walk and run in boy scout fashion back to Cheddington carrying the single line staff, without which no other engine could

Gates and crossing keeper's house at Broughton Crossing. When this photograph was taken in 1984 the rails had long been lifted. The little house still serves as habitation 140 years after the Aylesbury Railway had built it.

Bill Simpson

A warning sign for engines that are no more, a rail-less goods yard.

John Spencer

Overgrown cattle dock and despondent loading gauge hang above a trackless pathway on 1st June 1965.

John Spencer

After the end of train services altogether Marston Gate fell derelict. The lever frame protrudes from weedy silence with the gates rusted shut. The acetylene cylinders on the right belong to the line cutting gang, this melancholy task being performed in June 1965.

John Spencer

enter the branch. At Cheddington he was very interested to find that the engine available for the rescue work was a 4-4-0 ex-Midland Compound. Jack returned on the footplate to collect the stranded train and push it into Aylesbury. The rest of the day's workings were operated by the Compound. Upon examination it was found that the lame engine had blown away part of its blast pipe. The signalman at the time at Cheddington was Ken Hall who also recollected the incident.

"The usual turn of the Compound was to run up from Willesden light engine and collect the two parcel vans that were always on the last train up from Aylesbury and left in the middle siding at Cheddington. On this particular night the Compound collected the staff that Jack had brought on foot from the failed loco and went along the branch, buffering up to the stranded train and pushing it all the way to Aylesbury. It then collected the parcel vans from Aylesbury that should have been taken by the next train and took them to Cheddington but did not as normal roster would require, take them to Bletchley, so they were left on the middle siding at Cheddington whilst the Compound returned to stay at Aylesbury overnight and worked the passenger service the next day. It was well past midnight before the Compound went on shed. The failed engine was a Webb Coal tank, the Compound was No.41165."

Ken first knew the line in the 1950s and remembered that besides the normal afternoon goods there was space left in the timetable for a morning goods. The reason for this was related to the ability of Bletchley to hold the freight on its yard. There was often a lot of wagons for Aylesbury and this extra goods train would act as relief, the loading limit on the branch being fifty wagons. When a goods train came in with a big load like that the goods brake would be standing under the bridge at Dropshort, with wagons held on the crossing. What they did then was to uncouple the engine at the station, as the goods would be run into the station. The bolt would be released in the box for the ground frame so that they could switch the road to allow the engine alongside,

A photograph taken by the author in 1984 little realising that it would be amongst the very last to be taken of the station in this form. Shortly afterwards the building was sold and the timber section demolished, whilst the house itself has been altered beyond recognition. There is an interesting variety of sash and casement windows.

Bill Simpson

Marston Gate building as photographed in 1984 shortly before the timber building that housed the ticket office and block instruments was demolished.

Bill Simpson

reversing alongside to get behind the train at Dropshort, and coupling on the rear it would draw it back so that it cleared the points at Dropshort. Finally it would push the train over the crossing and into the yard.

During the winter of 1947 a passenger train worked along the branch with an ex-LNWR 'Prince of Wales' class at its head. This must have been the only time one of the class worked that branch! Certainly in later years there were LMS "Crabs", Stanier Moguls, Black 5s on passenger workings sometimes and one time the unrebuilt 'Patriot' No.5511 *Isle of Man*.

From a passenger's point of view F.G. Cockman of Bedford, who has produced numerous books and articles on railways, recollects his use of the line from 1939.

"I used the line about once a month between 1939 and 1945, when travelling between Bedford and Aylesbury. The locos were then Webb 2-4-2 tanks Nos 6601 and 6666. These two went all over the place doing work on the Bedford to Bletchley line, the Aylesbury branch and the Newport Pagnell branch. Passenger trains were not very full and I cannot remember anyone using Marston Gate station and, on winter nights its solitary existence was noticed only by a single oil lamp."

The canal basin at Aylesbury that saw heavy use practically up until the day the railway closed and competed successfully with loads not required in great haste. All canals passed into a limbo of neglect during the late 1960s and '70s. In later years they have been revitalised with leisure interest, thus the well stocked basin seen here.

Bill Simpson

The station at Cheddington in 1987 as an 'up' fast hurtles obliviously towards Tring Summit. The station still sports four platform faces with the trackless edge of the Aylesbury platform beyond the brick buildings on the left. From the station footbridge the tour de force of a modern main line is very impressive. It is interesting to compare this photograph with the view of 1873 on page 86.

Bill Simpson

Fireman Wesley Robins remembers bringing in the last train to be worked by men of the Aylesbury depot on the final day in September 1950 when it closed. As they entered the station with the last 'down' working of the day the Leighton Buzzard men were waiting to take the 2-4-2T back to Leighton, leaving the coaches at Cheddington. From then on the service would be run from there. His recollections of engines on the branch shows a varied assortment. The staple 2-4-2 5ft 6in tanks Nos 6604, 6618 and 6699 fitted with what he called a 'donkey pump' (LMS push-pull equipment), were replaced in the 1950s with the 2-6-2T engines. Variety came to be supplied by the afternoon goods which was by no means the preserve of six and eight coupled goods engines. A Class 3 ex-Midland 4-4-0 with 7ft wheels would turn out or three-cylinder engines from the 'Patriot' and 'Jubilee' classes, and he saw Nos 5500, 5504 and 5518 on this duty, bearing in mind that part of the working was to shunt the Aylesbury goods yard.

"Never seen anything like it trying to shunt a string of wagons with 'em exhaust ripping up and driving wheels flyin'."

There was some mixed traffic workings on the branch, an 11.00am and the 8.50pm were classified mixed, and these were allowed 22 minutes on the journey, rather than the normal passenger time of 15 minutes. The usual assembly was the passenger coaches, goods wagons and a brake van. Occasionally there were specials hauled by Black 5s with one of these coming as empty coach stock from Willesden. The train was hauled tender first from Cheddington then run round at Aylesbury. The train then took on its intended passengers which were thousands of troops being taken to Northampton for demobilisation.

Wesley Robins verified the unorthodox method of running round that seemed to be working practice for many years, but to what extent in the LNWR period has never been ascertained. That is, to run into the platform road first and unload all passengers, then uncouple. The guard would blow the vacuum so that we could give the coaches a push until they cleared the points. The engine was run onto the side road whilst the guard released the brakes and let the stock roll back into the platform under his control. The engine would then simply run off

Jack Turner, fireman on the branch during the late 1940s, stands with one leg on the running plate. Beside him is guard Aubrey Ewers and behind Arthur Waller. It was Jack who had to run to Cheddington with the staff after their engine failed mid-way. This introduced the rarity of a Midland Compound 4-4-0 working on the branch for a single day.

Jack Turner

the side road and back onto the train, facing the Cheddington direction. If the run-round loop outside the station platform area was used the locomotive had to go over the road crossing at Park Street, which made the driver very unpopular. Traffic was known to wait for 15 to 20 minutes whilst a particular engine shunted the yard. All the way up the street would be a convoy of about twenty brand new cars, one behind the other with their delivery drivers fuming. They were being delivered from either Birmingham or Coventry and they did not care to wait around as this was money lost to them.

Wistfully Mr Robins also recalled the fascinating directness of the line, so straight without any visual obstruction.

"Once you had turned the corner of the line at Cheddington you looked straight at Aylesbury over the smokebox front. I used to watch the distant Granada cinema neon sign growing steadily larger out of the winter darkness."

Signalman Len Kinchens who manned the Cheddington box from 1954 to 1965 recollected the times during the goods only period at that station.

"You see, they used to have all the parcel traffic come from Aylesbury that had to be transported over for the main line parcel trains, barrowed over the crossing at the Tring end of the platform to reach the 'up' slow. On Sundays they had all Wallaces' flowers, and normally they used to be loaded at Standbridgeford station but when that was closed on a Sunday they were brought to Cheddington. They used to grow mostly carnations in very long greenhouses at Eaton Bray. When the branch closed they stopped the parcel trains stopping at Cheddington so Wallaces had to take their flowers to Leighton Buzzard station. There would be three lorry loads at a time being taken to the station every day. At Christmas they would do chrysanthemums in bowls which provided extra trade. There were three signalmen for the Sears Crossing box. Also three signalmen at Tring Cutting box. They all came under Cheddington. There were two signalmen at Aylesbury and two porter signalmen at Marston Gate. Details of signalling at Mentmore: distant, three quarters of a mile in Aylesbury direction for 'up'. The 'down' distant was under the platform starter at Cheddington. On the frame was a lever to unlock the gates also."

Signalman Ned Goodyer of many years on the branch, pulls the levers over on the final day. In twilight shadows the goods yard is just visible through the window.

Bucks Free Press

Fireman Cyril Gibbins worked on all the lines radiating from Bletchley with the exception of the Newport Pagnell branch. His experience of the Aylesbury Branch however was after it had closed to passengers, when only the daily goods working would make the seven mile journey through rapidly overgrowing rails.

"It was like going on safari going down that branch in the last ten years. We could have anything for this working. I've known 'Patriots', 'Jubilees', Black Fives and "Crabs" do it but usually it was an ex-LNWR 0-8-0 class. From the Bletchley yard we followed the 12.40pm Bletchley to Euston passenger as far as Cheddington. From the slow line we would back into the middle siding between the 'down' slow and fast lines. You got across onto the branch when gaps in expresses permitted. In my time there was not a lot for Cheddington besides coal but when Twyford Seeds operated in the area we delivered wagons of 'shoddy' which was all manner of textile waste, even old suits. They had many wagon loads which they ploughed into the ground to help retain moisture.

This method of operating the gates at Mentmore in those final years was to send the porter from Cheddington.

There was a chap called Reggie Pollard, who used to get his bike and cycle round there whilst we waited in the branch platform. When he opened the gates he signalled to the box on the block bell in the hut and they cleared us through. Even though Reggie was crippled in his hand with arthritis he did clever little drawings of country scenes and animals all over the gateposts at Mentmore. This added to the attraction of an already attractive little crossing. On one side was an orchard for Buckinghamshire prunes, the fruits being very similar to a damson. The roadway leading up to the house had trees arranged in figures of eight. We had one disruption to the tranquillity that could have been nasty at the crossing. The Aylesbury goods was in the green card link at Bletchley which meant that you would have drivers retired from main line duties often with a 'passed' cleaner firing. On this particular occasion it was an ex-LMS Mogul, "Crab" and the young fireman wasn't doing too well. They got as far as Cheddington with the old boy helping him out with the shovel but when they got onto the branch they realised too late that they hadn't enough steam to put the brakes on and on she went round the corner and through Mentmore crossing gates. Not much chance for Reggie to cycle round for that one!

George Thorn, passenger guard alongside the branch line train at Aylesbury. The coach is No.07443 a brake/third introduced 1912, 54ft in length.

Lens of Sutton

Lifelong guard George Thorn hoists the last regular passenger tail lamp before the final journey back to Cheddington.

Bucks Free Press

The gates were closed behind us and Reggie would leave at about 1.30 or 2 o'clock. He would go back to open them when we returned at 5 or 6pm after Aylesbury had rung through to the box to tell them that we were on our way back. Any wagons for Marston Gate, which was pretty rare towards the end, would be brought back with us as they could only be dropped off by an 'up' train because of the position of the siding. There was quite a lot for Aylesbury though, coal, petrol, diesel oil and general goods.

Getting back onto the main line could be a real problem because the slow line would be pretty solid with the Bletchley residential services from Euston, I've waited for well over an hour to get on the line, after all, you could hardly have a Super 'D' trundling down the fast line with two dozen wagons in the rush hour could you!"

Chapter 8

The Final Years

Unglamorously shunting Aylesbury yard, 3-cylinder 4-6-0 of the 'Jubilee' class No.45722 *Defence* after bringing in the Bletchley goods on 28th January 1959.

Geoff Williams

With effect from Monday 2nd February 1953 the United Counties bus company brought in its revised timetable for route No.104 and 104A from Aylesbury, calling at Aston Clinton, Wilstone, Marsworth, Tring, Long Marston and Cheddington Green. Five return trips daily with one extra on Friday with seven complete trips on Saturday. There were no buses on Sunday. This replaced a direct train service of eight 'up' weekdays, nine Saturdays; seven 'down' weekdays, and nine Saturdays.

It is interesting to observe that with the closure of the passenger services on the Aylesbury line it was not to be succeeded with the inevitable scaling down of the goods service. The daily goods from Bletchley continued with varied and interesting locomotives filling in on this duty.

To give some indication a company called New Holland sent out of Aylesbury 40 trucks of agricultural machinery each day. The Shell Mex depot was also busy and the gasworks needed its daily allocation of a dozen wagons. There was also Silcocks cattle feeds, and in fact

Stationmaster E.C. Binch stated that he thought the goods side of the station business could be kept open for the products of Hazell, Watson & Viney alone. Horse and cattle trains were still in demand but it has to be admitted that these were not to be provided for in the forthcoming British Railways Modernisation Plan of 1955.

The station buildings were not demolished but were utilised as a store by a local wine and spirit company. With the closure of the signal box at the time of withdrawal of the passenger trains, the gates and points were operated by a gateman who travelled with the train which was restricted to a speed of 15 mph on the branch.

Undoubtedly the use of the crossing for yard shunting operations would be argued by those that wished to see it closed and the emphasis in the Modernisation Plan for brake fitted units hints away from the marshalling and re-marshalling goods system. Even many of the fifty yards planned for retention would become anachronisms with the advent of the Freightliner trains. Clearly

One of the last glimpses of Aylesbury LNWR yard before the track was removed in the early 1960s.

Southill Collection

with an alternative station in the town BR centred goods reception at this depot and on the 2nd December 1963 finally closed the old station. In the following year Dr Beeching enacted his transport remit and closed a hundred and six.

As the first weed strewn rails were clawed from their resting place in that same year it could not be compared with the dramatic requiem attending the nearby ex-Great Central line a few years later in 1968. They were lifted all the way back to Cheddington by May 1965 where they were still used as a long refuge siding. Occasionally, large locomotives like Stanier Pacifics dropped off vehicles with a hot box, contrasting mightly with what had once been the preserve of modest tank engines. The branch line platform was used by the police forensic team to work on the ill-fated TPO 'up' special from Aberdeen to Glasgow and Euston that was relieved of £2$\frac{1}{2}$ million pounds on the night of 8th August 1963 near Sears Crossing, just under two miles north of Cheddington.

The incident requires no further publicity here other than to pay tribute to driver Jack Mills who was badly beaten and died seven years later without ever recovering from the trauma of its effects mentally. A copy of *Railnews* of May 1984 raised the point that Jack may not only have had the train robbers to deal with but his engine was also the harbinger of misfortune. Eight months before No.D326 had been involved in a collision north of Crewe in which 18 people died and 33 were injured. The year after the train robbery a man working on the locomotive's roof was electrocuted by an overhead power line and in 1965 a guard was injured when it ran out of control on the approach to Birmingham New Street. Little wonder that as No.40126 it was allowed to pass to the scrap heap unmourned.

The resignalling of the main line with multiple aspect signalling took place in two stages. Stage 1 was from

Wolverton No.2 to Stoke Hammond 'up' lines and from Leighton Buzzard No.2 to Wolverton No.2 'down' lines took place between 10.00pm 26th June 1965 and 5.30am Monday 28th June. Stage 2 between Stoke Hammond and Cheddington and between Leighton Buzzard and Grovebury Crossing took place between 10.00pm on Saturday 3rd July and 5.30am Monday 5th July.

At Cheddington the signal box was defunct, together with all running signals north of the box and replaced with multiple aspect signalling. The crossover between the slow line once used by trains going onto the Aylesbury line was worked from a new ground frame electrically released from Bletchley power box.

Although the Aylesbury line is heavily overgrown in parts a few traces of its existence remain. At the time of writing, in 1987, the site of the station is predictably utilised as a car park. Few drivers will realise that they park their vehicles on the foundations and cobbles of the original station of 1839. The much vaunted by-pass road to dissect Park Street planned in the final days of the goods workings has still to be realised. A few osiers still grow at Stocklake and the factory building that used them now acts as a store. Remarkably at Broughton Crossing the tiny London & Birmingham crossing keeper's house has not only survived but is still occupied alongside a pair of gates.

For a time after closure the Marston Gate station house was disused but was then re-occupied. After being sold in 1984 it was altered beyond recognition, but the letterbox still refers to Marston Gate Station.

Beyond Marston a permanent way hut, No.8 stands apparently without purpose amongst rolls of hay. At Mentmore the hedges that once enclosed the trackbed still reveal the width of railway land, far wider than the track itself and of course purchased for the unrealised development of separate 'up' and 'down' lines had the Aylesbury branch been extended.

The yard at Cheddington has been completely cleared

Bob and Peter Williams sitting on the crossing gate at Mentmore in September 1957.   *Geoff Williams*

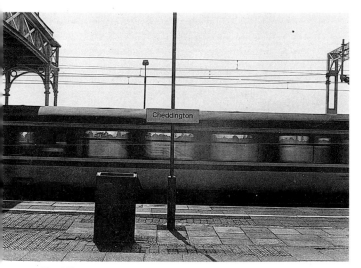

Cheddington 1987.   *Bill Simpson*

In the November twilight veteran porter/signalman Jack Rogers pulls over his levers for the last passenger train on the branch in regular timetable working. He had spent all his working life at Marston Gate. The frame consisted of six levers 'down', distant and home – points and gatelock – 'up', distant and 'home'. Note the Annett's keys for gatelocks. To open the gates for road traffic again he must first put the signals to danger, lock the frame and take out the keys which he inserts in appropriate positions on the gatelocks after moving them back across the tracks.   *Bucks Free Press*

once again in acquiesence to the motor car although the fogmen's cottages and the stationmaster's house still survive. The age they represent contrasts dramatically with the electrifying bursts of speed and frequency of main line trains passing through Cheddington station now.

In 1988 this line was 150 years old. By comparison with its first trains of unfortunate exposed passengers the present travellers ride in virtual palaces on wheels at average speeds of over 80mph. Their journey time of under two hours for a normal service train compared to five hours between the two cities in 1838 would be beyond the wildest imaginings of a mid-nineteenth century mind.

With regard to branch lines, largely speaking they have passed into history, with all that is left of the Bletchley network being the 16 miles to Bedford Midland. Although the twelve miles from Oxford to Bicester has recently had its passenger service reinstated.

Happily the town of Aylesbury still has a vigorous train service to both Marylebone and Paddington, but like the first station, passenger trains now terminate in the town. At least in an age that has seen many towns divested of their railway services, including the former county town of Buckingham, it is something to remain thankful for.

Epilogue

by Geoff Williams

A view of Dropshort in 4mm scale on Geoff Williams' superb model of Aylesbury station. A ballast train is passing through on its way to Cheddington.

Geoff Williams

It was about 35 years ago, when looking for an example of a vertical screen at a small LNWR station, that I "discovered" Aylesbury. Here was the perfect example of a glazed screen and more, much more was all the North Western atmosphere. I decided that all this was too good to ignore, it was a complete LNWR backwater and would make an excellent subject for a model.

The layout was to be in the LNW period and built to the scale of 4mm to the foot and 18.2mm gauge track. As the model progressed prototype information was continually being collected from numerous sources including the local library and museum, the Bucks Herald, local people especially, coal merchants, and, of course ex-railwaymen. All this research was, and still is, at times very exciting. I shall never forget the many happy times I had with George Thorne, one time guard on the branch and a veritable mine of information. More recently I had the pleasure of meeting Mr. Cartwright the son of the dairyman on his float featured on a photograph in my collection dated about 1915. He still has the original float from which I was able to discover the correct colours for my model.

As time went on much of this information showed up many basic inaccuracies in the model especially for the period I was trying to portray. There was only one thing to do. Start again! It is this second model, Aylesbury Mark II that was started about 25 years ago and is the subject of these illustrations. Over the years it has become quite a "family affair".

Hopefully, most of the original shortcomings have been eradicated in the later version. The track layout is correct for my period and all railway buildings are to scale length although there had to be some shortening of sidings etc. Of necessity much of the background scenery has to be a compromise but I have tried to produce the atmosphere of the original. Park Street, North and Randall's and the High Street shops were subjects of some study but by far the most dominant feature had to be the gasworks. Southern Gas were very helpful and provided a works plan.

In conclusion I would like to acknowledge the help on railway matters I have received from the Historical Model Railway Society and the London & North Western Railway Society.

Aylesbury station with branch trains at the platforms. 5ft 6in tank No.910 and three 30ft 1in carriages. The gasworks is in rear with High Street shops and Exchange Street in the far background.   *Geoff Williams*

A ballast train leaves the yard hauled by Coal Tank No.252 showing the engine shed (called "Steam Shed" in the LNWR period) with the end of Norfolk Terrace in the right background.   *Geoff Williams*

A general view of part of the coal yard with the goods yard in the background and the gasworks purifiers on the left.

Geoff Williams

The irritating habit of Langdale Brook overflowing the road and cutting off Marston Gate Station is recalled by Christine Dunker.

Langdale Brook

The brook, they said, had overflowed,
For all night long it rained and snowed
And blocked with water was the road
To Marston Gate.

The angry clouds were black and blue
And Mail, it seemed, was overdue
For Postman wasn't getting through
From Marston Gate.

The train, if running, would be late–
No train at all could be the fate
Of those who had to sit and wait
At Marston Gate.

And climbing high on sloping bank
We braved the snow on bending plank,
And spirits sagged as high boots sank
Near Marston Gate.

But finally the trek was made
For horse was bold and unafraid,
And trap was high, we swung and swayed
To Marston Gate.

And in came 'Flier' hissing steam
With firework sparks and piercing scream–
And was it true–or just a dream–
Of Marston Gate?

Coal Tank No.252 approaches Park Street Crossing, showing the right hand side of Park Street. One of the gates at the entrance to the basket works is open.

Geoff Williams

Park Street again, showing left hand side and signalman's cottages. Stocklake is in the foreground.

Geoff Williams

The station forecourt and High Street shops with North &
Randall's premises. (An early photograph before the scenery
was completed.)

Geoff Williams

Christine Dunker recalls the local commuters view of
Marston Gate.

Poet Christine Dunker departs form a bleak Marston
Gate.

Goodbye Marston Gate

The road was bleak, the hedges starkly bare
With icy flakes in frosty morning air
And we exhausted, wearily we strode
Down winding stretch of stony Marston Road
A two mile walk for early morning train
When cry would be 'She's running late again'.

She always was, we sat by fireside heat
With fingers numb and chilblains on the feet
And asked for papers, 'None' was terse reply
Of he who viewed the shrouded sullen sky
And watched through mist of wreathing ashen hue
For signs of smoke as monster came in view.

We heard and saw–vociferous the cries
With slamming doors and eager watchful eyes
Of those our friends who indicated seat
As whistle shrilled and hustled lagging feet
And we inside, we heaved contented sigh
And leaning back, waved Marston Gate goodbye.

Marston Gate

There really was a station–Marston Gate–
With early morning gloom if train was late
When passengers would huddle round the fire;
No morning papers, nothing to inspire
The roving eyes, save battered wooden clock
Precisely stating time with tick and tock
Until the noise was drowned by piercing scream
As train arrived with hissing spouting steam.

A sudden rush, no waste of precious time,
The doors flung wide, and high athletic climb
To smoke-filled carriage, dimly dark and grey,
With corner seat, and crumbs of yesterday.

Then eyes would peer, would watch for black-faced sheep
In distant meadows where, from wakened sleep,
They scattered wide as monster hurtled by
Disrupting peace, with smoke-disfigured sky.

A rhythmic change, a rushing hustling speed,
And silence fell, a strain to watch and heed
The banks of weeds, the hedges bristling thick
With coloured leaves, ripe blackberries to pick;
Then going slow, terminating tossing,
Red for danger, nearing Broughton Crossing–
Points manoeuvred, sight of Aylesbury town–
"We're nearly there–be careful stepping down."

Index